Life's About A Dream

A Memoir

By Veda Rogers

iUniverse, Inc.
Bloomington

LIFE'S ABOUT A DREAM
A Memoir

Copyright © 2012 by Veda M. Rogers.

All rights reserved. No part of this book may be used or reproduced by any means, graphic, electronic, or mechanical, including photocopying, recording, taping or by any information storage retrieval system without the written permission of the publisher except in the case of brief quotations embodied in critical articles and reviews.

iUniverse books may be ordered through booksellers or by contacting:

iUniverse
1663 Liberty Drive
Bloomington, IN 47403
www.iuniverse.com
1-800-Authors (1-800-288-4677)

Because of the dynamic nature of the Internet, any web addresses or links contained in this book may have changed since publication and may no longer be valid. The views expressed in this work are solely those of the author and do not necessarily reflect the views of the publisher, and the publisher hereby disclaims any responsibility for them.

Any people depicted in stock imagery provided by Thinkstock are models, and such images are being used for illustrative purposes only.
Certain stock imagery © Thinkstock.

ISBN: 978-1-4759-0546-5 (sc)
ISBN: 978-1-4759-0547-2 (ebk)

Printed in the United States of America

iUniverse rev. date: 03/21/2012

Merrily, Merrily, Merrily, Merrily
Life's about a dream!

Kathryn Age 3

Chapter One

On January 13th, it was Friday the 13th, they realized they were at the end of their five-year plan. It was necessary to define new goals for the next few years. Planning was easy for her; she often sat at the calculator for hours punching in different numbers to see the effect on the bottom line. Her job in the business was to manage those numbers and she considered that time important. They had been running the summer theater for eight seasons. Some seasons broke even; most ended with red ink. It wasn't too bad, because with their winter jobs they were able to keep the theater going without much ill effect. If the bottom line could include the impact which summer theater had on the economy of the rural area where it was located, or the rising young artists being nurtured, it might prove to be a profitable venture.

"Oh, but you have a lot of fun," the local customers would say when inquiring if the theater would be open again next year.

"Well, we don't have much choice, do we? We have too much invested to stop."

Fun? She remembered the feeling of terror each June knowing there would be no stop until after Labor Day. Not terror because of fear, but certainly some dread mixed in with a lot of anticipation. There was just so much physical work involved, long hours and little privacy, the summers were not something she looked forward to as "fun." Satisfaction would come later, perhaps, in the form of applause, or a feeling that the play had gone well, or a company that got along, or a full house, or—dream on—money left over after paying all of the bills.

The theater was located in a barn. In the country. The nearest town of seven hundred was seven miles away. There was a lake close by, which, at the onset of the theater, had averaged fifty to a hundred thousand visitors each weekend. They had based their decision for that location on those particular lake statistics. "If just one percent of the campers come to a show, that's between five and ten thousand people! We can make a go of it with that base."

The barn had a sort of prominence in the landscape, on a rise, easily viewed from both directions. The young couple had taken a drive to the lake in search of the right spot to locate a theater. When they saw that barn, it was obviously vacant and they both knew it was right. They pulled into the driveway and started to get out of the car.

"What do you think you'll find in there?" his mother asked, "Nothing in there but stanchions and stalls." They both got out of the car anyway and were followed by Maggie, the nine year-old. They had to brush aside dry weeds taller than the daughter. It was August and the summer had been dry, but the vegetation had grown to a height half the doorway. The door had evidently not been opened for some time, it was rusty and gave much resistance. Once inside, the three found an old harness hanging on the wall. It smelled of the horse who'd worn it years before. There were stanchions and stalls and a small room on the northeast corner which was probably once a grain bin. The dirt floor was packed hard and smooth from the many years of hooves, feet and equipment. There was also a loft, which was about half full of prairie hay that had been cut earlier in the summer. They climbed the ladder to the loft, she handing up the daughter to him. Once on the floor of the loft, he did a "shuffle-off-to-Buffalo" routine and shouted, "Hey!" with his hands splayed awaiting applause. They noticed windows on the south side and climbed upon a bale of hay to look out. The view was expansive. He pointed to a tower on the left saying, "That's Williamsburg over there."

Downstairs the south entrance had a sliding door which opened easily. Outside that door was a barnyard full of weeds. The barnyard overlooked the highway. The parents stood there looking both directions for a few moments before entering the barn again and closing the door to go back through the back entrance to return to the car.

His mother asked again, "Well, what did I tell you?"

"You were right, Mimi," he said, "Just stanchions and stalls."

Maggie piped up, "Those would make good dressing rooms, Daddy!"

They had not told the children about their plans to start a theater, not that they wouldn't involve them. It was inevitable that they become involved. But when Maggie made that statement, the parents realized the children already knew what was on their minds.

"Are you going to start a theater?" Mimi asked. "If so, that's not the place to do it. It's just an old barn!"

"Exactly, Mother, just what we are looking for. Do you know who owns it?"

"Yes, a Mr. Poertner; he lives across the road. He and his wife used to live in the stone house here. I sold her Avon. Then, when the lake went in, Doris and Glen's house was moved just across the road and they sold it to the Poertners, she's Glen's sister, you know. Glen and Doris then moved to Pomona and built their new house."

He wondered if Mr. Poertner would be interested in selling the place.

* * *

The next day they drove back out to the lake. It wasn't far from Mimi's house in the little town of Quenemo. They had both grown up in Quenemo and, although the area had gone through many changes with the lake, a federally funded flood control project, they were both in familiar surroundings. Her father had been part of the Kansas delegation to lobby in Washington, DC, for flood control. That was during the fifties. Whether due to his efforts or not, Congress approved the appropriations for such projects to be completed throughout the whole country over the next twenty years. Pomona Lake opened its gates and banks in 1964. Because it was the first of the planned reservoirs to open in the proximity of Topeka (30 miles) or Kansas City (75 miles), the influx of campers, boaters, fishermen, etc. was immediate. During the summer of 1966, on a brief camping trip shortly before the family had moved to their home in Winfield, they stopped overnight at Pomona Lake. The campsites were literally butted up against each other. Vehicle bumpers were two to three feet apart. It seemed more congested than a big city. They both agreed they would never go camping again, if that were what "getting back to nature" was all about.

They looked around the barn again. This time they also looked at the rock house. A stone in the west gable was carved, "1876." She whistled, "Ninety-three years old!"

The yard had two cherry trees full of dried up cherries. On the east side of the house, there was a garage. He said he could put in partitions and make a bunkhouse for housing the cast. Other buildings on the property included a dilapidated lean-to chicken house "possible storage" and a foundation in the barnyard which looked as if it might have held a long narrow building, but which had been torn down or moved.

They drove to the lake to see how many visitors that weekend held. Lots of cars. Lots of campers. Sailboats splaying their colors on the lake. Motorboats with skiers. They then drove to the house across the road from the barn to visit with Mr. Poertner, the owner. They knocked at the back door of the white farmhouse and waited. Just as they were about to leave, the door opened. "Mr. Poertner," he began, "I'm Bruce Rogers. My wife and I have noticed the place across the road and wondered if you own it."

"Come in," the man said. As they followed him through the back porch, passing the kitchen and on into the living room, they realized why it had taken the man so long to answer the door. He wasn't such an old man, maybe seventy something, but he was so crippled. Walking or any kind of movement seemed to be a struggle for him. He made an apology for the disorder of the house; he had "arthuritis," he said, and didn't clean very often. The house did not appear disorderly really. There were places to sit, and plenty of room to move around. They both said it looked fine.

"Yes, I own that place. My wife and I lived over there until the lake went in. Then, we bought this house from my wife's brother and moved it to this spot. It used to sit down by the Hundred and Ten Creek Bridge.

"Sure, I remember it now," Bruce said, "My dad was the mail carrier from Quenemo when I was a child. Sometimes he would take me along on his route which included delivery of the Vassar mail."

"Your father?" He asked. "Would that be John Rogers? I remember him, and your mother, too. Used to deliver Avon to my wife. She always looked forward to her visits. How is your mother?"

That is the way it is with a small community. It takes a while to get to the core of a visit. You must establish who you are, your kin, where you lived. Maybe it is no different from city talk, not having lived in a city before, she could not say. After they became acquainted and the couple had learned his wife had since died, they told him they would be interested in purchasing the property. He said he couldn't let them have the whole piece, as the parcel to the north had been sold to his wife's sister in Topeka, and she and her husband had re-platted their acreage into building lots, but there were roughly thirteen or so acres still available in the corner fronting the highway. He wanted to know what they would do with it.

"We thought, maybe, a summer theater."

"Well, there's not one of those around here. It might be all right. I'd have to talk to my boys first. I'll give you a call in a couple of weeks and let you know what they think."

That night neither of them could sleep. They sat together on the bed of his old bedroom in his mother's house and began plans. They started making a budget and schedule of what would need to be done to get the place ready to open as a theater. Who could do it? Where would they get the money? How much would it take? They could sell their eighty acres of farmland in Western Kansas. His grandmother had given it to them for a wedding present. They had used the property as collateral many times. It had been mortgaged two different times to purchase a car, then as down payment on their home in Junction City, and more recently, to provide the down payment on their home in Winfield. Sell the farm? How could they tell his mother that? That was her home. Of course, it was just a small piece of the farm, his mother still had the major part of the property where her father and his father had farmed for over a hundred years.

The reason they had come to Quenemo that particular weekend was to attend a music reading session held by the Wingert-Jones music store in Kansas City. His mother had offered to tend the children so both of them could attend. Before leaving for KC the next day, however, she telephoned her brother in Topeka.

"Hello, Dick? It's Veda. We are in Quenemo, going to Kansas City today, but we have something we would like to discuss with you and Ruth and wonder if you will be home tomorrow. We'd like to talk to you."

"Sure, we don't have plans. Come on up."

Both were groggy from lack of sleep and it was difficult to sing. Participating in the choral reading sessions had become an annual event, one they both looked forward to. They would often encounter old friends from college who were also in the field of music education. Plus, the sessions always provided new music and ideas for him for the coming year. It was usually beneficial both for the music store and the teachers. This year, however, when the breaks came, they didn't look up their old friends; rather, they would meet in the hall outside the reading room to discuss more theater plans. Excitement was high.

After the music reading ended, they headed downtown Kansas City to meet with some friends from Wichita. John and Carole Lynes were their oldest, closest friends. They met them as planned in the restaurant at the top of the Commerce Tower. John had been in KC all week for a computer training session. He worked as an accountant for a small milling company in Wichita which had just installed, or was planning to install, their first computer. In 1969 the computer age was just beginning for the small business. No one knew how to run the contraptions; yet the owners realized a computer was going to be a necessary fixture for their company's future. John was studying the new languages of Basic, Fortran and Cobol.

At dinner the couple divulged their theater plans wondering if their friends would laugh at them, try to discourage them (there was no way either of them could be discouraged), or what. In reality, however, their news fell on very receptive ears. They were encouraged. After all, what are friends for?

John and Carole remained in Kansas City for the night, while the would-be entrepreneurs drove the 75-mile trip back to his mother's house in Quenemo. Although they were still excited and wanted to make more plans, the lack of sleep from the previous evening had caught up. Weariness won in the end.

The next morning the sounds of the children came early from the adjoining rooms. His mother had a large house with four big bedrooms upstairs. The two girls shared a room, while Chris was able to have his own room. Mimi had more than a normal share of talent for homemaking. She knew how to wallpaper, sew curtains and upholster furniture. And her baking—she made the best lemon meringue pie anywhere, her only son always boasted. So the house always held a cheerful welcome. She loved having the children come to visit, and they adored their grandmother. They also loved Twiggy, her little red and tan Dachshund. Twiggy was the runt of the litter of the children's female Dachshund, Heidi. They had another Dachshund, Juliet, who was the mother of Heidi. When the family went to the grandmother's, they usually took their dogs along; so the house would ring with the noise of three children and three dogs. Kate, the older daughter, was ten that summer. Maggie, as stated earlier, was nine and Chris was eight. Stair steps.

The couple told Mimi they were going to go to Topeka for the morning, but would be back early afternoon to visit before going back home to Winfield. She said she would take the children to Sunday School and Church and give them dinner. It would be some time before she would be able to have them for the weekend again.

Dick and Ruth were in their kitchen when the couple arrived. They lived at the edge of Lake Shawnee in an old two-story rock house which they were renting. When they first moved in, the house had been vacant for years and it needed a lot of work to make it livable. The sweat was provided by Dick and Ruth. No equity, however. They had tried to get permission to purchase it, but due to the owner's living in California, permission was never granted. It would be several years before they would resign themselves to moving to a house they could buy.

"Dick, where did you get the car?" Bruce admired an old Chevy parked in the drive.

"Like it? I've got an option to buy it. 1937, the year I was born. I'd like to get it, but I don't know. It needs a lot of work and Ruth doesn't think we need it."

They entered the kitchen door. The kitchen had been the latest remodeling project. It boasted barn siding on the walls, and an iron spiral staircase leading to the second floor. It was the first Veda or Bruce had seen the new kitchen, and they were much impressed. The stairs led up to a room off what had become the master bedroom. The little room was formerly a storage closet, but Ruth had convinced Dick it would make a comfortable dressing room. After the tour, the four found Sara, eighteen months, sitting in her rocker watching a local Sunday television show for children where Whizzo, the clown, would read the comics. Sara watched with rapt attention.

"Sara?" her mother called as she passed through the dining room where the television was located, "Your Aunt Veda and Uncle Bruce are here. Don't you want to say hello?"

The toddler raised her left arm in salutation without turning from Whizzo.

"We'll be in the kitchen, if you need us." She waved again.

The four adults sat around the kitchen table. "A theater? What's brought this on?" Dick asked.

"Well, we've been giving ourselves to community theater for eight years and we've decided we should try doing it for profit." Veda related their trip to Colorado from which they'd just returned. She told of attending the melodrama at the hotel in Cripple Creek and another small theater near Green Mountain Falls where they had stayed at Gibson Corner for a week. At Cripple Creek they had seen *The Count of Monte Christo*. The stage appeared to be all of eight feet square at the most, and the cast of five or so doubled many roles. At the end of the show, they all bounced back on stage for a half hour olio where the actor who had played the title role in the play sang a Noel Coward number, *Have Some Madeira, m'Dear!*, singing nearly the entire number to Margaret who was practically sitting on the stage, the audience also in a somewhat limited space. Maggie's nine year-old frame was dressed in her best dress, white tights and black patent leather shoes, with her long ash-blonde hair shining in all of its glory. This added to the comedy of the number and the audience was very pleased.

The cabin near the foot of Green Mountain had been offered them following the 1969 summer Winfield Children's Theater production of *Kanorado* for which Veda and Bruce had written the music, the orchestration and the direction of the show itself. The piece was an embellishment on his father's creation of many years prior. Set in a small community on the western Kansas border, the town is divided when a new survey proves the state border running down the center of town. Half of the town becomes part of Colorado and the other half remains in Kansas. This divides the town, not only geographically, but also, the women and girls stay on the Colorado side while the men and boys keep residence in Kansas. His father, John L. Rogers, had put the play together in 1955 using many of his old songs and writing some new tunes. The work had the potential of a Cecil B. DeMille epic, with a long tent revival sequence, a train trip across Kansas and a pancake race similar to the annual Shrove Tuesday event between the towns of Liberal, Kansas, and Olney, England.

Veda had taken the original work, called on her neighbor, Kay Kirkman, across the street to write a new book and dialogue, and together they had written a musical with some new songs and a new story. It kept to the original plot in that the city was still divided, but being set around the time of World War I, the division was not due strictly to geography, but also, included the women's suffrage movement and the emotions of war.

The two friends had worked days, evenings and weekends through the spring, bouncing ideas back and forth until they felt they had a show that children would be able to play, yet still appeal to an adult audience. The Winfield Community Theatre gave the event the attention of a first-class world premier. There were photo spreads and interviews and rehearsals from which Veda would return home to work on a late night revision to a song, cutting, writing new material, which Bruce would later have to orchestrate. All of this while trying to maintain his full time teaching position and Veda's after school private voice lessons, plus the daily routine of household chores, the laundry, cleaning, shopping and room mother activities.

During the final week of rehearsals for the premier, Betty, the matriarch of the Gibson family, had come to Veda and said in her velvet baritone voice, "You need a vacation. We want to give you the keys to our cottage in Colorado." It was absolutely the nicest thing anyone had ever done for the family.

Back in the kitchen at Lake Shawnee the two couples were discussing the possibilities of forming a partnership. Dick said he was ready to make some changes in his life. "In fact, that's why you see the '37 Chevy sitting in our driveway. I have been contemplating a new project. Maybe the theater would be just right."

Chapter Two

Later that evening parked in front of their own Winfield home, the family unpacked the car and moved luggage, dogs and vegetables from Grandma Driver into the house. After raising nine children, Veda's mother found it difficult to break the habit of planting large gardens or preparing meals with two vegetables, a meat, potatoes, salad and at least one dessert. And she remained of slender build, never weighing more than a hundred and twenty pounds at her heaviest. No one could ever visit her without taking with them something from her harvest or kitchen.

The house at 501 East Eleventh was a large three stories with full basement Queen Anne which the couple had purchased upon moving to Winfield three years earlier. When Bruce learned he had the job of vocal music instructor for Winfield High School, they had brought the children to Winfield for a weekend to look for a house. After viewing several newer homes and insisting they wished to purchase an *older* home, the realtor showed them the Kyger house. The front door greeted the visitor with a leaded beveled glass window. Inside, to the right there was an oak Victorian carved staircase leading to the second floor. On the left stood two massive ten-foot columns creating the entrance to the front parlor. The realtor showed them oak sliding pocket doors leading to the other parlor where there was a fireplace and a built-in bookcase. This room adjoined the dining room which boasted a Tiffany style chandelier and a built-in china cupboard with a pass-through to the kitchen. The realtor explained that the house had been built before the turn of the century and the lady who owned it had died recently. Mrs. Kyger owned a furniture store downtown. The Kyger family had lived there a long time, but he didn't know when they had purchased the property. The couple stood visiting with the real estate agent when the three children raced one by one in through the front door, up the stairs all the way to the 3rd floor attic, down the back stairway to the basement and back up to the first floor by way of the front basement stairway. Christopher, who was then five, shinnied up one of the columns, raced outside where he collected a couple of snails discovered in the side yard and came back to his mother saying, "We've decided we want to live here!" The parents were convinced. Later on, after they had moved into their new home, they learned that the Kyger family had purchased the property around 1910 and it was there that they raised their two daughters, Catherine and Margaret. Ominous.

The family began redecorating the house one room at a time, and in that particular summer of 1969, following the production of *Kanorado* and their Colorado holiday, the master bedroom was the next room on the list. Wallpaper and paint had been selected and ordered. Fabric for new drapes had been purchased and another material obtained to make a coverlet for the walnut bed. Mimi had arranged with a lady in Quenemo to do the quilting. In fact, Veda had taken the fabric to the quilt lady on that weekend trip, and for the next two weeks, while Bruce and the children were preparing for school, she was to peel away the old paper, prepare the woodwork for a new coat of "Antique gold" paint, which more resembled a shade of avocado green, and sew the matching draperies. He would come in to paint the ceiling and help hang the wallpaper. Their division of labor was clearly defined.

They didn't discuss their new plans with anyone. First of all, it wasn't settled whether or not they would be able to purchase the property and second, Ruth and Dick had not made up their minds to join the partnership. They had said they would think about it for a few weeks. Plans were for Dick and Ruth to spend the Labor Day weekend in Winfield with Bruce and Veda and they would make their decision at that time.

The last week of August, the Winfield Community Theatre held auditions for "Hello, Dolly!" Bruce had been selected to direct the show, and he had spent quite a bit of time reading the script, playing the score, making notes and plans for the production during those weeks after they returned home.

"You're going to audition for the role, aren't you, Veda?" he asked after reading the script and then roaring with laughter as he recited the stage directions for the *Motherhood March*.

"I'm not sure I should. There are so many others who want to do it and after spending so much time on *Kanorado* this past spring, I don't know if I want to go into rehearsals again so soon!"

But, once the evening came for auditions, a new excitement soared. John and Carole and their boys, Steve and Scott, were down from Wichita. John had come to the decision there was more to life than pushing a pencil, and he wanted to audition for the chorus. And Carole, a talented flutist in her own right, offered to play in the orchestra.

Veda listened to friends read for Cornelius and Minnie Fay and Mrs. Malloy. Then, Bruce called for Worall Clift, owner of a local shoe store, to read the part of Horace and for her to read Dolly. She couldn't help herself. She had not yet even read the script, but when she saw the lines, it was as if Thornton Wilder's character spoke to her or through her, "Eat your beets, Horace, they're good!" "I'm going to get married again, Ephraim; I'm going to rejoin the human race." She wanted to play Dolly.

The following Labor Day weekend they were joined by Ruth and Dick who drove in from Topeka. They had decided to become part of the theatre venture and the partnership was formed. Dick reported that they had driven to the lake and viewed the barn and the other buildings. But when Bruce mentioned converting the garage into a bunkhouse, Dick responded, "I didn't see a garage, did you, Ruthie?"

"There was a cement pad and foundation just east of the rock house that might have once been a garage."

"But I remember seeing a garage there—a wide one, just two weeks ago!" Bruce insisted.

"Not there now."

Ruth asked, "When is Mr. Poertner going to give you an answer?"

"He said he would call this weekend."

On Saturday the two couples attended an auction of furniture and fixtures of the historic Bretton Hotel which was being razed to make way for a new building. There were beds, desks, dressers and some tables. It was surprising, for the hotel was a hundred years old and the items for sale were all 1940s and 1950s pressboard. Nothing of beauty, thought Veda and Bruce. Ruth, however, was thinking about the theater even though she didn't know for sure there would be one, and she said she thought they ought to buy some bureaus and tables.

"We'll keep account of the money out of pocket and settle up later."

After making a tour of the building and the basement, Bruce found Veda standing in the lobby and said, "I've found what I want. Do you know what you want?"

"Yes," she said.

"What is it?"

"I'm looking at it." She was gazing at the pressed tin ceiling fourteen feet above them. It was made of two-foot square pieces of deep molded tin.

"That?" he asked, "You want the ceiling?"

"Uh-huh."

"Come. Let me show you what I want." He took her down a flight of steps to the basement and into a room where stood a painted icebox. It was huge with five doors and was six feet tall or more.

"This is insane," she quipped, "It's ugly, dirty and it must weigh a thousand pounds! How do you ever plan to get it out of this basement?"

"Bruce force!" he answered and flexed his forearms. He scratched a spot on the side of the piece and said, "Look, it's solid oak and it still has its original hardware!"

"Solid, all right. Okay, you can have the ice box if I can have the ceiling. Come on, Let's ask."

They looked up the auctioneer who was handling the sale.

"Ice box? Where? In the basement? Oh, that! We were just going to bury that thing with the debris from the building. Do you know if someone wants to move it out?"

"I do. How about six dollars?"

"Sold! Pay the cashier over there and tell her what it is. You have to get it out of here latest on Monday. The building will be torn down on Tuesday."

"My wife wants to buy the ceiling. How much?"

"Oh, I can't sell that; you'll have to talk to the contractor who is tearing down the hotel. Leonard Richardson."

"Sure. I know Leonard. I'll give him a call." They paid the cashier, joined Ruth and Dick and left.

Once home Bruce telephoned the contractor who said, "Sure, you can have the ceiling if you're willing to take it down yourself." Leonard promised he would call him when he needed to have it removed, as he would be working on the top stories of the hotel for a few weeks.

Later that evening the telephone rang. Veda answered it.

"Mrs. Rogers, this is Frank Poertner. Your husband there?"

"Yes, I'll call him." She rested the phone on the desk and in a breathless voice called to Bruce on the side porch where he was sitting with their guests enjoying homemade ice cream.

"Bruce, it's Mr. Poertner." The three other partners ran into the parlor to listen.

"Mr. Poertner, this is Bruce Rogers. Oh fine. Yes, a beautiful day. You have? Good. All right. Okay. Well, thank you for calling. We'll be in touch." He hung up the phone. Turning to the other three, he cleared his throat, grinned broadly and sang from *Annie, Get your Gun,*

"Let's go on with the show!"

The rest of the weekend the four spent their time setting priorities and defining the tasks each was to accomplish over the next few months. Dick was going to see to the mowing of the property and cleaning it up. Bruce and Veda would find a buyer for their western Kansas property and pick a weekend to drive out and get it sold. Dick and Ruth would contact a lawyer to have a partnership agreement drawn up and also, to contact Mr. Poertner's lawyer to make arrangements for closing the sale.

On Monday, Labor Day, Bruce contacted several friends to accompany him to the Bretton Hotel. Veda fixed dinner for everyone while they made their way to the hotel to move bureaus, tables and the ICE BOX to the garage. The ceiling would have to wait. Over dinner the four partners announced their plans to start a summer theater at Pomona Lake. Sitting around the table with them were Wayne and Jane Cherveny, John and Yvonne Eckert, Carolyn and Dick Harrison and Don Gibson.

Carolyn had planted the seed for the Winfield Community Theatre three years before. She was a singer with strong desire for performance; so, with her young toddler, Joe, in arms, she went from door to door of her friends and acquaintances stirring up interest. By her efforts the Winfield Community Theatre was formed. While living in Junction City a few years earlier, Bruce had served on the board of directors for the Junction City Little Theatre. He volunteered to obtain their articles and bylaws and help charter the organization for Winfield. Carolyn was able to pique the curiosity and interest of other citizens, and in August of 1967, the group announced that the first show, *Guys and Dolls*, would be performed the following October.

Veda served on the search committee to locate a site for the theatre and the round barn at the fairgrounds had been selected. It was owned by the city. A request was made and permission granted to use the barn for one show. It didn't matter that the electrical entrance was insufficient to power high wattage theater lights or that there was no backstage. The place was a show barn! Cattle and other livestock were led onto the scales and into the arena, where they then exited through a chute into the barn area. The search committee, Don Gibson, Lucille Matthews, Kent Collinson, Jean Warren and Veda discussed ways to make the place work. They all agreed there was a charm to the space. The playing area was not in the round, but rather, a sort of thrust. The stage was lower than the audience. Actors would need to be trained to look up at their audience, rather than out, as would be the directions for a conventional proscenium stage. It would be as if playing from an orchestra pit. Don Gibson suggested that other risers could be brought into the center chute so as to be able to seat more persons. They also discussed using the loft for the orchestra, giving the actors additional incentive to look up. The orchestra would sit behind the audience. The conductor would have the advantage of seeing both the stage and the pit (or loft, in this case) and the actors would be able to have a good view of the conductor. The problem of not having backstage was one they would not be able to solve. The actors could exit downstage left or right by just walking "up" the aisles of the audience, or down center by exiting through the cattle run, but how were they to have upstage entrances or exits? They would need to enter from the outdoors. Perhaps the middle of October might still be warm. Maybe it wouldn't rain.

They took their ideas and concerns to the other charter members, and, in spite of any drawbacks, the barn was selected to be the performance space for *Guys and Dolls*. Auditions were held the end of August. In the cast were Carolyn as the Mission Doll, Sarah Brown, Wayne Cherveny as Sky Masterson, Veda in the role of Adelaide with Kent Collinson as Nathan Detroit. Don Gibson was cast as Harry the Horse. The rest of the cast was a cohesive mélange of Winfield citizens and the backstage crews were just as varied and interesting as the actors. It was a happy group of new friends. The lack of backstage space was solved with a horse trailer and a makeshift lean-to constructed of plastic sheeting tacked over some posts to keep out the wind. And, there was wind! October's blue, blue sky turned dark, dark gray with an early norther. With no heat in the building, even the audience was cold. The Hot Box girls in their skimpy nightclub costumes had to have coats waiting for them as they warbled, "Good-bye now!" to the audience, and exited upstage right (out into the rainy Walnut River valley). "Coats! Blankets! Wrap me up in something! A tent! Hand me some of that plastic!" It was cold. The chill, however, didn't dampen the enthusiasm for the new civic project. The sold-out-every-performance show was a hit and the theater bug had bitten a lot of new performers.

evd Winfield

* * *

"Why choose Pomona Lake for your site?"
"When will you open?"
"What shows are you going to do?"
"Are you moving to Pomona?"

The new partners were barraged with questions, many of which had no answers. They admitted that they were embarking on a new adventure; not one of the four had any sense of business. They didn't know how to determine the price of a ticket. But they knew how to work. They knew how to put a show together. Dick said, "I know how to plumb the bathrooms." They thought they could meet the deadlines and provide a product the public would want to buy.

Chapter Three

"Bruce, can you come up here for a minute?" she called from the upstairs makeshift office in the back hall. Every fall and spring she would pack up the files and equipment and move everything to Vassar or Winfield, whichever the appropriate season. It was a major move twice a year, but the family had become quite adept after eight seasons. The past season, Summer 1977, they had played *Annie, Get Your Gun*, the John Patrick comedy, *Everybody Loves Opal*, Gilbert and Sullivan's perennial favorite, *The Mikado*, Neil Simon's *The Star Spangled Girl* and *The Music Man* by Meredith Wilson. The season had gone well. Quite a few company members had returned from the previous season and their growth and maturity showed. Each year audience members would ask if this or that player were going to return. They especially loved to renew acquaintance with Eleanor Richardson and that season Bruce had chosen *Opal* specifically for her. She *was* the quintessential Opal, a favorite with the company as well as the audience. She had first joined the summer troupe in 1972 as General Cartwright in *Guys and Dolls*. On his way home from school one early spring evening that year, Bruce had encountered Eleanor at Albertson's Grocery and asked if she wanted to play the General for a couple of weeks. She did! She then moved her Winnebago from Winfield to Vassar, parked it on the cement slab where Bruce had once envisioned a bunkhouse for the players, and hooked up her power cable to the pole Dick installed especially for her camper. She became entrenched. Her first summer, 1972, she brought along her two teenage daughters, Ann and Beth, who also joined the mission band. As the run of *Guys and Dolls* neared its end, Beth asked to stay on for the summer and her mother agreed. She took the extra bunk in the Rogers' home, the red trailer.

By the summer of 1977, the management had taken a shift and Ruth and Dick were no longer part of the partnership. It was just Bruce and

Veda's operation. They had expanded the venture in the spring of 1974 by purchasing a steamboat, which had been built for the lake several years earlier. It was a sixty-five foot double-decker, rear paddle wheel, steam-powered riverboat. A Methodist minister at Lyndon had built it about the time the lake opened, and he and several others ran it on weekends as an excursion boat. Bruce and Veda had ridden it several times, taking friends who might be visiting, and on one occasion they had chartered it for a midnight cruise as an end of the summer cast party.

The Whippoorwill Showboat

Upon hearing that the owners were planning to move the Whippoorwill Steamboat from Pomona Lake, the couple decided to purchase it and offer cruises with a dinner and show. By its fourth season, 1977, the boat had become quite popular. It was open to the public four evenings a week, Thursday through Sunday, and available for private cruises the other evenings. Although they would sail on Mondays, they usually tried to steer a private cruise to a Tuesday or Wednesday so as to give the troupe Mondays off.

Preparing both the dinners and shows had become a component of the daily schedule for the players. Housing and meals were a part of the pay for each company member, and kitchen duty and cleanup were expected in their daily chores, as well. Scheduling was a task for the management. They had to plan menus for the company meals as well as menus for the meals to cater to the boat. And, of course, they had to schedule time for rehearsing and building of the shows both at the barn and boat, as well as time for cleanup and box office/telephone duty. With the hectic schedules, keeping the company morale could become a problem. When attending spring auditions and meeting with prospective actors for the season, Bruce would always emphasize the close living quarters, the lack of privacy, no personal time and stressful schedule. He would say, "A summer at Vassar will help you to decide your future. You will love it and decide to stay in theater, or you will get out before you make a big mistake!"

Somehow or other, it was working. During the winter months, while still maintaining their jobs and family activities, the family continued to remain involved in the winter schedule of the Winfield Community Theatre, which by then had a full winter schedule and was playing in the original barn that had been renovated into a comfortable, heated space with real theater seating. The couple spent time planning the following summer season each fall with consideration placed on the audience poll from the previous summer. After eight seasons they had not only developed a strategy for knowing exactly where their audience lived (they did a car count each evening, checking license plates for the county of location), but also, they knew how many persons per car. They had kept records of audience numbers by night, by show, by type of production; musicals were always the favorite or at least the best attended, and by temperature and weather. Their audiences would complain about the heat, but, within reason, as the temperatures lowered, so did the audience numbers.

The summer heat was a problem for the barn. They had talked of air conditioning "some day." Once during 1975 they even brought in a heating and cooling firm from Topeka to advise, but the idea of sheet rocking the walls to accommodate insulation did not appeal to the owners' aesthetic tastes. "We like the looks of the original barn siding." So, cool air had not yet become part of the five-year plan.

"What have you been doing up here all this time?" Bruce brought his wife a glass of wine and sat down with her.

"The annual reports; the W-2s are done and ready to be mailed to last summer's employees. I've cleaned the files and packed 1977 away. The cabinets are ready for another year. And I've also begun tabulating numbers and projections for next year."

She had the month of January off from her teaching position at Southwestern College, and had learned to make use of that month to develop most of the projections and budgeting for the next season based upon the pre-season ticket sales. They offered special season ticket prices for the Christmas season each year, and it usually netted a good base for beginning the next spring. This year had been particularly strong for pre-season sales and thus, her projections were up.

"We have come to the end of our five-year plan. We've added housing," her reference was to the yellow trailer, brought to the premises in 1975, which the couple now shared as their summer home with the office and catering kitchen, "Added a communication system between the barn and the boat, a sidewalk to the bunkhouse and a concrete slab on the north side of the barn for shop space." They didn't make big plans, but they aimed for some annual progress.

"What have you been thinking we need to do?"

"For one, I'd like to have a real kitchen," she responded, "It gets harder and harder catering the boat meals from our crowded yellow trailer. And I don't like battling the vermin of the rock house kitchen any better than the cast." They talked of possibly moving a boxcar in to be converted into a kitchen.

He said, "You know, refrigerator cars are well insulated. One of those might adapt to a kitchen and company dining space real well." He began to think of other uses for a boxcar, "We could use more storage space."

As they continued to discuss whether they needed one, two or three cars, Bruce's eyes started to twinkle as he exclaimed, "How about a whole train?"

"Are you serious?" she asked.

"Yes, a whole train! We can use the caboose to open a bar; we can make some passenger cars into a restaurant and use boxcars for storage."

"Please, Bruce, I don't want anything else that moves." She was referring to various problems they'd encountered with their steamboat. Although the boat provided a charming evening for the customer, it was always a challenge for the cast and crew. Performing in the open air meant battling summer gnats and mayflies as one tried to maintain character and poise. Also, it meant being careful not to inhale them as you sang. And, the weather was always a concern. What might be a welcome breeze at the playhouse would appear to be a gale in the middle of the lake when the boat was broadside the wind. Salad would literally blow out of the bowl as the stewards were trying to serve the meal.

Also, the tape recorded music was powered by a steam generator, and it was a rare performance that the generator maintained 110-volt power throughout the evening show. One might be singing in the key of C and suddenly the key would rise and the tempo increase, or slow and the key lower to a drone. The actors were always instructed to keep a sense of humor and help the customers to have a good time regardless of the technical difficulties. And they did.

She reiterated, "NOTHING THAT MOVES!"

"No, it won't move. The train can ring the playhouse. We can bring in a depot. What do you think?"

That evening, Friday, January 13, 1978, was the beginning of a new project for the couple and it was every bit as exciting and wonderful for them as the one begun eight and a half years earlier in the summer of 1969. They talked and planned for several hours. Often their voices were raised to the point of waking the children, all of whom were home for the weekend. Kate was by then a sophomore at Southwestern College; Maggie was a freshman at Emporia State University and Chris, a junior at Winfield High.

The next morning the children asked, "What were you and Dad doing last night? We could hear you laughing, shouting and talking. What's going on?"

Chapter Four

For years Veda had been saying that they should keep a diary. Oh, she had kept an activity calendar and numerous schedules for various shows, but what she wanted was a real diary. Something to not only track the events of her life, but also, a place to log any thoughts pertaining to the day or event. So, after Christmas that year, she had purchased a diary. Christmas had brought both Mimi and Grandma Driver to visit for the holidays. Mimi was a usual guest for special events, but her mother had to divide holiday time among Veda's seven living siblings (she had lost a brother in Germany during WW II), so a Christmas that included Grandma Driver was extra special. Kathryn had made the trip to Quenemo to pick up the grandmothers on Friday the 23rd.

Bruce and Veda had decided to give their mothers a family photo for Christmas; thus, on Christmas Eve, after the mothers had gone to bed, they summoned the children up from the television room and told them it was time to get ready. They all dressed in their finest of the day, Veda and the girls in long skirts, which she had sewn an earlier Christmas, and Bruce and Chris in their best suits. Veda set up the tripod to hold the camera for a time shot and the family posed in front of the Christmas tree. After taking several shots, she retreated to the basement to develop and print the black and white photos, while Bruce and the kids finished wrapping their gifts. She had already purchased frames for the photos, and after the development and printing process was done, she dried the prints, framed them and wrapped the gifts.

Veda had discovered photography a couple of years earlier and found that she liked being in the darkroom with its chemicals and amber work light watching a print come to life. The decision for her to learn the skill was made when, one summer, 1975, a photographer did not come through with his product. It was a disappointment to not have photos of that season and her reaction was simply:

"Hell, I can do that!"

So, when fall came, she made several trips to the library to pick up books on photography, the processing of film, making the prints, what equipment she would need to buy and what work would need to be done to create a darkroom. After a few weeks, she announced, "I'm ready to order the equipment. Bruce, you can build the darkroom now."

A corner of the basement where there was a cast iron sink had been chosen to house the darkroom. The old basin was removed and replaced by a used two-bin porcelain kitchen sink. Once the construction was complete and the newly acquired equipment was installed, Veda shot a roll of black and white film to practice her new skill. She sent that roll to be commercially processed and then, made prints from the negatives to see if she could duplicate those commercially made snapshots. She prepared the pans of developer, stop bath and fixer, put the negatives in the enlarger and began. She was surprised that the darkroom felt so natural. Although she would set her timer as the textbooks advised, she would always find herself unconsciously counting during the periods of development and printing. And, a few nights later she had a dream that found her at an enlarger with another photographer (or teacher) giving instructions. The black and white photo enlarger was a huge Bessler that she had never seen before. The dream was so vivid and clear that upon arising the next morning, she recited it to Bruce.

"I was wearing a long skirt and high necked blouse, peering into the lens of this enlarger. I remember once actually being in the darkroom of The Eitner studio in Ottawa, but I don't remember seeing any of his darkroom equipment—just the pans of chemicals. The funny part is—I could swear the instructor in my dream was Stan Reimer."

Stan Reimer, a former band instructor at Winfield, who had found a hobby in photography, had given up his teaching career to establish a photo studio in another Kansas town. He had come to Vassar a few times to do the season's shots and the players had all found his work to be excellent. Had he remained in Winfield or moved a little closer to the playhouse, they would have asked him to continue shooting their summer shows. Alas, he had moved too far away for such trips to be mutually cost effective.

Why had she dreamed of Stan? And how could she know such detail of that obsolete photo processing equipment? It was several months before she saw a drawing, to remind her of that particular enlarger from her dream, in a book on the history of photography. And the wheels of her imagination ran rampant with the possibilities of reincarnation and the idea that maybe she had already experienced work in a black and white photo laboratory. And, was Stan Reimer her mentor in this other period of existence? Well, who are we if we're not at least a composite of those who have come before us—chemically, physically, and yes, even telepathically? That thought satisfied her curiosity from further probing.

The family photo of Christmas 1977 was a surprise to the mothers. They asked when it could have been taken; they knew Margaret had come from Emporia along with them only the day before. The girls were able to explain that Santa works in mysterious ways. Several years earlier on Christmas Eve their parents had moved them out of their bedroom as they slept, and set up a whole new bedroom including a canopy bed with curtains, a vanity with matching skirt, a new book shelf unit with dresser and electric sconces. When the room was finished, the parents carried their sleeping daughters back to their bed so that they might awaken on Christmas morning in their new room with a canopy bed.

The prep work for that new room had been done all during the month of December in the guest room. The parents had kept the door to that chamber closed and told their children not to go in, as it was Santa's workshop. And, the children believed it. In fact, as they listened to the pounding and sawing in the "workshop," they thought their folks were making a Christmas surprise for Mimi. The couple found that the only drawback to that particular Christmas present was their fatigue the next morning when the girls were delighting in their present. They were too tired to enjoy the surprised looks on their daughters' faces.

Another Christmas, the parents prepared a program, which they presented to their family and Miss Karr, their neighbor who lived in the little house in their back yard. They worked up an interpretative *pas de deux* to the Fred Waring recording of *'Twas the Night Before Christmas*. They spent their evenings after the children had gone to bed with choreography and rehearsal. Then, on Christmas Eve they donned matching flannel nightshirts and caps, put the record on and gave their performance of the poem as set to music by the popular singing group.

In early December of 1977, Kathryn had participated in Southwestern College's production of *Amahl and the Night Visitors*. It was an annual event for the family to watch the opera on television, and Kate was always the first to get the recording out to hail the advent of the Christmas season. Some years the Christmas season at their house began as early as September!

"No, Kate, don't play that yet!"

But she liked the opera. Veda and Bruce realized early that their first daughter had a special talent for music. Once, when she was about three years old, Veda had boasted to a friend about her daughter's ability to pick out tunes on the piano.

"Not only does she play the tunes, but she plays them in the key she's heard them."

Veda's friend, Jan Starr, (another music teacher), nodded unimpressed. Later on, however, when the two young women were in the kitchen singing a snatch of *Somewhere Over the Rainbow*, Kathryn was then heard playing the same melody on the piano in the same key. Jan subsequently admitted, "Now that's impressive!"

So, during the Christmas season of her first grade, when her daughter came home from school singing the opening oboe melody of *Amahl* and Veda had asked her where she had heard that tune, Kate answered. "Oh, this morning we heard *Amahl and the Night Visitors* in school. Would you get me the record?" After one listening, she could sing that long opening melody.

Kate transferred from KU to Southwestern in the fall of 1977. She had attended her first year of college at the University of Kansas, "majoring in Hashinger Hall," according to her parents. Living at the performance residence hall was her life at the university. There she found friends and the opportunity for performance, as she was cast that year in major roles of two Hashinger productions, *Dames at Sea* and *The Apple Tree*. Kate had a passion for performance and she would persistently argue with her parents to allow her to quit school and head for a large city to seek a career in entertainment. Why go to class? She candidly admitted that she was not attending classes at KU, and she begged her parents to let her transfer to a smaller school if they wouldn't let her quit her studies. Her parents finally agreed, and at Southwestern she was able to maintain a performance schedule and still go to class. Her grades were showing marked improvement and she was doing well with her studies of violin and voice.

She auditioned for *Amahl* that fall with the intent of capturing the title role in the production. She had memorized the entire score years before and was ready. It was, therefore, a disappointment for her when the role went to another student, but realizing the importance of the chorus in any production, she agreed to be in the ensemble. Veda played piano and coached the singers for the production, and rehearsals were rigorous. The director, Norman Callison, head of theater and director for the annual summer Horsefeathers and Applesauce productions of Southwestern College, began rehearsals with the idea of flying ropes out of the ceiling of Messenger Theater for some of the shepherds and peasants to make their entrances. He envisioned other ideas, which for one reason or another were never realized. Evidently there were other frustrations for him, as well, because during the final dress rehearsal, at an early point in the evening, he became so enraged over some actor's entrance or response to a line or some other infraction which seemed minor even at the time, that he stormed out of rehearsal before the cast had completed even the first few minutes of the evening's work. Ah, the artistic temperament at work . . . . Veda stopped the piano, came onto the stage and asked what had happened. The cast and crew all shrugged unknowingly. "Well, we have a show to do," she said, "and I suggest we get busy and get it done!"

The rehearsal continued with the stage manager taking over and the show did go on as intended with the director back en force the next evening. They played two performances. Veda could always recognize and appreciate Kathryn's clear soprano voice leading the Shepherd's chorus. She did not overpower or stand out, but her solid knowledge of the piece and her acute pitch and intonation were just what the group needed as they came from the lobby making their a cappella entrance up the aisles of the audience.

* * *

At Christmas of 1977, Veda began her diary. She was determined to keep it faithfully, maybe not each day, but definitely each week. At first, the entries were reports of routine activity: closing the books for 1977, preparing a budget for 1978, and other annual tasks. As the spring progressed, however, she began reporting trips to Sedalia, Missouri to look at retired railroad passenger cars and plans for expanding the barn to enclose the shop on the north and add a covered patio on the east and south. Also included for that spring of 1978 was an entry pertaining to the couple's decision to resign their teaching positions and take on the Vassar project full time.

"That will mean selling our house and moving to Vassar full time."
She was very reluctant to leave Winfield. Memories flooded her thoughts.
"When shall we give notice and put our house on the market?"

At first they talked of doing the project in a couple of stages, taking two years before they left their jobs and their Winfield home. After further discussion, the time line was cut to moving in one year after Chris had graduated. Then Bruce said, "Why don't I give notice tomorrow and we can move on Tuesday?" Not too realistic! It was finally decided to move at the end of that school year.

The remainder of January was spent with Veda wallpapering the hall and back stairway. Margaret was still on January break and she helped her mother by painting the steps and woodwork. In February, Maggie returned to Emporia and Veda began her final semester of teaching at Southwestern. Maggie had auditions for an ESU production of *Peter Pan* upon her return to school, and she was cast in the ensemble. The show was scheduled for early May.

Winfield Community Theater was, in the meantime, in rehearsal for *The Sound of Music* and Kathryn had been cast as Liesl. It was also scheduled for early May, and to compound the situation even further, Bruce was directing the high school production of *L'il Abner*, which opened the same week as *Sound of Music*. What a week! Kate had a college chorus and orchestra concert on Monday, in which she sang the soprano solos in the Vivaldi *Gloria* and she also sang Adele's Laughing Song from *Die Fledermaus*. Following the concert, she fled to the barn to catch the end of her dress rehearsal for *Sound of Music*.

Sally Wright was Maria. Sally had married Rick Rottschaefer two years earlier and they had returned to Winfield after living in Houston for a year. Sally and Rick. Rick and Sally. They met at Vassar in 1973. Rick designed the set and played Cornelius, with Sally as Ermengarde, in *Hello, Dolly!* A Vassar romance. For her audition in the spring of 1973, Sally drove to Winfield wearing two-inch platform shoes with bell-bottom pants. She sat at the piano in the front parlor and sang *Who Are You Now*, from *Funny Girl*, and Bruce and Veda both thought Barbra Streisand had just entered their lives.

Veda, Sally Wright and Joe Burgess. *Hello, Dolly!* 1973

They had known Rick a little longer. He arrived in Winfield in 1971 as a freshman at St. John's College and, before he'd unpacked his grip at the dormitory, he heard of auditions for *The King and I* at the Winfield Community Theater and left to seek out the barn at the fairgrounds. He was cast as Simon Legree in the show within a show, *Small House of Uncle Thomas*. Bruce was the director for that production and Veda choreographed the ballet. From their very first meeting, a bond was forged and Rick began spending his evenings at the Rogers house, sometimes babysitting. Once, he even re-glazed the beveled glass window in their front door while house sitting when the family was away on vacation. Rick was to spend more time than any other player over the next few years at Vassar, so much more, in fact, that Bruce eventually dubbed Rick his first son. He would explain that this was because he was older and taller than Christopher.

1973. I had to "kick on" the lights for my entrance—everyone else was on stage!

Sally first moved to Winfield to attend Southwestern College in January of 1975. She was cast in the spring 1976 Campus Players production of *Company* with Rick in the role of Bobby. They were married in May 1976 with plans to spend their honeymoon at Vassar. Bruce and Veda were fraught between wanting, indeed, needing them to participate in the summer season and persuading them to either wait until the end of summer to marry, or, to not do Vassar that summer. They knew that Vassar could tear apart relationships as easily as it could shape them. But, Rick and Sally decided to do the season at Vassar. The 1976 summer began with *Oklahoma* at the barn. Rick played Will Parker and Sally was cast in the boat show, *An American Jubilee*. The turnover found Rick on the boat directing *Pirates of Penzance* and Sally at the barn playing Gooch in *Auntie Mame*, with Veda in the title role. Sally was also Veda's backstage dresser for that show. There were some nineteen costume changes. All were choreographed and the costumes were preset in a specific order with Veda under dressing wherever possible. The period was 1929 to 1940's and the vintage costumes were fragile. During one hectic change, Sally had the dress, a black one, ready as Veda popped offstage. She stripped rapidly out of her dress and Sally slipped on the new costume with one hand and strung a necklace around her neck with the other. As Veda was adjusting her hair to return to the stage, Sally noticed a hole in the right skirt seam of Veda's costume.

"Veda, you have a huge hole in your dress. Quick, let me sew it up."

"There's not enough time." With that she grabbed a can of black hair spray, lifted the skirt of her dress and sprayed her right thigh, hose and under pants jet black. She then proceeded to the stage with the flare of character requisite of Auntie Mame.

Carolyn Harrison had remained with the cast that summer following her role of Laurie in *Oklahoma,* in order that her son, Joe, might be cast as Auntie Mame's nephew and *little love*, Patrick. Carolyn sang in the ensemble for *Pirates of Penzance* aboard the Whippoorwill. She and 10-year old Joe were staying with her parents in Admire, not far from Vassar, during the run of those shows, and one afternoon prior to an evening's performance, she motored to Topeka to pick up her husband, Dick, who'd flown in from Denver to catch his son's performance. While en route to the airport, Carolyn had a serious auto accident, rolling the car and pinning herself under it. Joe was also in the car and, although uninjured, he was terrified that his mother had been killed. Her arm was badly cut and she had other bruises and abrasions, but she was alive! She was not able to make that evening's performance, but Joe did! He was later than usual getting to the theater, but no one in the audience could tell by his performance that anything out of the ordinary had happened to him. A trouper!

So, with the end of *Auntie Mame* and *Pirates*, Sally, who had become increasingly frustrated at having no time with her new husband, left the company and went home to her parents in Topeka. Rick had been scheduled to design and play the Emcee in *Cabaret* later in the season with Sally cast as Sally Bowles. It was a tough decision, but Rick decided to support his wife and quit the company for the season, as well. The newlyweds then moved to Houston where Rick obtained a job as an elementary school teacher.

Rick and Sally weren't the only newly married couple at Vassar that season. Donna and Steve Hailey had met as students at Southwestern College and they were married during the spring semester of their senior year. Donna Buffalino had appeared as Josephine in 1974 for the Whippoorwill's maiden voyage, *HMS Pinafore*, and Steve had also appeared at Vassar that same summer when the company traded shows with Horsefeathers and Applesauce who brought their production of *Once Upon A Mattress* to the Vassar audiences. Still, they were not considered a "Vassar romance."

* * *

The spring of 1978 progressed rapidly with what seemed to be considerable accomplishment. Kate was able to complete her activities for the semester as planned. In addition to being in *Sound of Music,* she had also been cast in the role of the aunt in Lillian Hellman's *The Children's Hour* which the Campus Players presented the previous March, and in which Sally also appeared as her niece.

Christopher's spring was full of wrestling meets and other school activities, including working on the crew for *Li'l Abner*. He was undecided as to where he should finish high school. He toyed with the idea of attending school at Quenemo, which was his parents' alma mater, but as fate would have it, the school had its final high school graduating class in 1978 before the Quenemo district merged with Melvern to become the Marais Des Cynes Valley School District. Going forward, high school students from Quenemo would be bused to Melvern, and the building which was completed in 1961, would serve solely as an elementary school for the consolidated rural school district. When Chris learned of that fact sometime later in the summer, he decided to move back to Winfield to live with the family's next door neighbors, Vic and June Martin, so he could graduate from Winfield High School.

The couple worked on the physical plans for the new project, meeting several times with various contractors; one, to construct the bed for the railroad tracks and another, to build the addition to the barn. They also made contact with the Missouri Pacific Railroad to purchase a caboose and three passenger cars, and they contacted the Santa Fe to purchase a third passenger car to house the players and three boxcars to be used as storage. Each day brought excitement along with problems. The problems were usually connected to money.

"How are we going to make this work if we don't get a loan?" Bruce asked one evening after they had been turned down for a loan by a second bank.

"Well, we have enough gathered together to purchase the cars and pay for the railroad bed, but we don't have the money to set them on the tracks. That may take some time," Veda responded. The couple had borrowed on some cash value life insurance to raise that money. They also cashed in some mutual funds, which were not growing at the rate that was touted when the couple had begun the investment five years earlier.

Enough of that, they had a summer season for both the barn and the boat to get underway. Although they planned to continue looking for funding, they knew that the sale of their house would surely provide the funds to complete the setting of the railroad cars—the vintage deplorable looking cars might have to sit undecorated a few months until they could scrounge up the money to complete their plans. At least they could begin the project on their own.

Chapter Five

The 1978 season opened with *Fiddler on the Roof* at the playhouse and *Dames at Sea* on the boat. During the spring Veda had made contact with a representative from the Kansas Economic Development Commission and had extended an invitation to the commissioners, along with representatives from the Department of Parks and Recreation, the Vassar State Park officials and families and other such dignitaries and representatives to attend a special evening aboard the Whippoorwill on Wednesday, June 21st, midsummer eve. The priority of the 1978 season was a new paint job for the boat and the purchase of some new folding chairs for the passengers.

The players were expected to help with maintenance; it was scheduled along with the preparation of the boat meals, costumes, properties, box office, set construction and rehearsals for both shows. The schedule was so tight that minute changes would mean some inconvenience on someone's part. For this season, there were several players returning from other years. Tom Mitchell was selected to direct *Fiddler*. He had first come to Vassar two years before to appear as Curly in *Oklahoma* and he was to return the next three years. Besides the family members themselves, also returning in 1978 were Larry Pressgrove, Jim Olson, Roger Aday, Eleanor Richardson, Julie Krieckhaus, Diana Gish and Jennifer Warner.

Jim Olson was chosen to direct *Dames* and play the role of Lucky. The others in that cast included Maggie as Ruby, Kate as Joan, Larry Pressgrove as Dick, and Tom Mitchell, besides directing *Fiddler*, played the role of the Captain in *Dames*. Newcomer Linda Waltz, as Mona in *Dames*, completed the cast. On the boat was Aaron Gragg, who was serving his second year as Engineer. Stewards who returned from the previous year were Debbie Kramer and Paul and Patricia Redding. Debbie's sister, Tina, joined the crew as a first time steward. Debbie, Tina and Aaron were all members of Quenemo's final graduating class of 1978, and Veda and Bruce had grown up with their parents. The cast and crew for the Whippoorwill were all seasoned except for the pilot, Bernie Wonsetler, who first came on board in May. He was a student at ESU and came to the playhouse by way of his acquaintance with Maggie. Because technical theater was his primary interest, she talked him into joining the company to wear both the hat of Whippoorwill Captain and that of heading the barn's technical crew. The night before his appearance, a storm had caused the boat to come loose from its moorings snapping some cables. Bernie's first morning was baptism by fire. He learned how to change the cabling and move the spars.

"Bernie, this is something you and Aaron will be doing on a regular basis, as the level of the lake rises and falls. This is as good a time as any to learn what to do." Veda gave him the first instructions regarding his job.

The boat was docked at the wharf boat, which was essentially another boat tethered to the shore. It was constructed as one, but it had no means of propulsion. The wharf boat cabin had space for storage of the tables and chairs and tools that would be needed for running the steamboat and moving the moorings. The process of landing the Whippoorwill was to cut its power approximately 100 feet from dock and coast along side the wharf boat. Then, someone from the cast or crew would jump off the boat as it came along the dock and throw out a rope from dock to another person on the boat. They would then wrap the rope around a cleat and pull it to a stop. Although it was a 50,000-pound craft, it was easy to pull over water. There was one time during the summer of 1974 that the boat had blown across the cove during high winds and the next morning, very early, Bruce and some of the players dove into the lake and literally swam the boat back to dock. That particular storm, August 17, 1974, happened while Bruce and Veda were in Kansas City attending the annual Wingert Jones choral reading session. They had completed the day's singing and had just stopped for a leisurely, quiet dinner before heading home to Pomona Lake, when Bruce said,

"I think I will call home to see how everything is."

"No, don't do that—eat your dinner and then, you may call if you wish." They had noticed a bank of light clouds in the southwest sky, but it didn't look serious.

Bruce called anyway and Rick answered the phone,

"It's okay, Bruce, we're all okay."

"What do you mean—you're all okay?" Bruce asked him.

"Well, we had a horrible storm that blew the barn off its foundation."

"Come again?"

"And we all went to the cave, so everyone's okay."

Needless to say, the couple cancelled their dinner order and left before another word.

"Bruce, you know Rick—he must have been exaggerating. That barn has been there nearly a century. It will be all right! And what about the boat? Did he say anything about that?"

"Yeah, he said it came loose and is now on the other side of the cove."

"Did it damage any other boats?"

"Hopefully not, I don't know."

On weekends the cove was usually full of small watercraft, because that was where the marina was located. Besides the normal services of fuel and supplies, the marina also moored some boats on a monthly basis. Because the Whippoorwill was located in that cove, the owners had to pay a percentage of the gate receipts to the Marina each month. It was a bone of contention with Bruce and Veda that they did not receive services for the monthly fee. The boat did not use gasoline—it was a steam engine and the boiler was fueled by diesel fuel. As for servicing the shifts in the level of the lake, Bruce and Veda moved the boat every time the lake rose or fell. Lawrence Stadel, owner of the marina, was married to Bruce's cousin, Pat Logan, but that relationship did not lower the percentage of receipts the couple paid each summer month. They knew Lawrence would probably have something to say to them when they got back to Vassar. He never was too kindly toward the Whippoorwill anyway, and if it went careening across the cove and struck any of the boats he was tending, there would be more than the regular fee to pay!

Their fears mounted when they reached the little town of Pomona and saw big trees that were cropped in half. It was as if they had been chewed by an enormous animal or machine with huge teeth. The vegetation continued to look ravaged the remaining ten miles to the playhouse. As the owner of a neighboring nursery was later to say, "You can replace a house, but a 100-year old tree can never be regained in one's lifetime."

Indeed, the barn had shifted on its foundation. Bruce didn't think that it was in a dangerous position, but the weekend performances of *The Fantasticks!* were cancelled in order to have someone with better knowledge assess the situation. The Whippoorwill had not damaged any other boats on the lake, thank God, and getting it back to dock was fairly easy. The production of *Luv*, which was playing on the boat at the time, was unique in that its setting is on a park bench near a bridge. In the course of the play's action, one of three characters jumps off the bridge in a suicide attempt. On a conventional stage, the actor would usually jump off a platform at the back of the stage into a pit where someone would throw water on him and he would climb back up, presumably over the bridge. On the boat, however, realism was possible. The actor would indeed jump into the lake—then climb back up over the paddle wheel and on up over the railing. No need for someone to splash water on him, he was dripping wet! That particular season was unseasonably cool, even cold during the run of the show and the audience shivered along with the wet actor. The chill also cut into the audience size.

Mimi arrived at the playhouse shortly after Veda and Bruce returned from Kansas City, with the news that her cottonwood tree had blown down. It didn't strike the house, but her back yard was a major mess and she was frantic not knowing how she would get it cleaned up. Bruce took a crew to Quenemo the next day to solve that problem. He found the tree splayed across her large back yard resting its boughs against her clothesline.

"This was a huge tree and look at it now!" Bruce related to the crew that he had planted that very same tree as a junior high student shortly after his parents had purchased the house. Cottonwoods, which are very common in Kansas, typically grow pretty fast, a fact which makes them, in their mature years, probably more vulnerable to high winds than slower growing trees, but this one had a trunk that was easily thirty or more inches in diameter. It had been there almost thirty years and must have expanded its girth by more than an inch per year.

With the help of a borrowed chain saw, Bruce and the crew were able to clear away the limbs, leaves and twigs that afternoon. It was a greater struggle to right the barn, of course, but, after a thorough inspection by a contractor, it was determined that the barn was still structurally sound and, with the help of the boat's "come along," the barn was slowly coaxed back into its rightful place and the season continued its course.

Chapter Six

The schedule for 1978 included an original show on the boat, *Ring Around Rogers*, a review of the songs of Bruce's father. John Logan Rogers had worked at different careers during his life: an insurance salesman, a newspaper editor, postmaster, and finally, rural mail carrier. But, he was always a composer regardless of which career was paying the bills. As a rural mail carrier, he would think up tunes as he drove his vehicle from house to house. His union with Myrtle (Bruce always called his mother, "Mimi") was a second marriage for him and he was almost 48 years old before his son was born. His first wife brought a small daughter, Virginia, into their relationship. John loved her as his own child, giving her his name, and provided the talented child with original songs for her to perform. Her mother, Lela Owens McMath, would pen the lyrics while John created the melody and rhythm. One song, *Cowboy Cabaret*, was performed for a c.1925 Charleston contest by the budding teenager while the family was living in Ft Worth, Texas. She won the contest and the first prize was a season on the vaudeville circuit. John left the insurance business to manage her act and the actress went on to become Ginger Rogers! Lela and John separated in the late 1920's and Ginger already had several movies to her name when John divorced her mother to marry Myrtle in November 1931.

Life's About a Dream

Ginger Rogers and her troupe sitting at a railway siding awaiting the train for their next gig in 1927. John L is back row on far right. Lela is next to him, and Ginger is beside her mother.

Bruce had known about Ginger all through his childhood, John L being very proud of the success of his talented step-daughter, and although her career didn't allow time for much contact, the actress did write her "Daddy John" and also, Bruce, from time to time, as he was growing up. Although the separation was apparently amicable, John used to say that Lela needed much more than he could provide. He would say that he brought home good money as an insurance salesman, but "Lela would carry it out the back door in bushel baskets."

Ginger Rogers Abt. 1940.

The young girl was very fond of John L and, when he died in 1960 at the age of seventy-three following a long battle with emphysema, Ginger sent a large spray of yellow mums that covered the upright piano in the Quenemo Federated Church along with a card that said, "To the only Daddy I ever knew, from your daughter who loved you."

Veda had contacted Ginger during the early spring of 1978, to invite her to come to Vassar and see the original show, *Ring Around Rogers*. Ms. Rogers responded that her schedule would keep her out of the country during the month of July, but she wished for a recording from the show, if possible. Veda was to assemble that show, choosing mostly John's tunes, but also, she planned to include some of the new songs she had penned for *Kanorado*. She and Bruce would plan to perform in the show as well. She had packed carefully to keep the music easily accessible, so as to begin putting the show together as soon as the season got under way.

By the end of May most of the cast had arrived and were well into their daily shifts of rehearsing and building the first show of the season.

The cast for *Fiddler* included some returning players, Jennifer Warner as Golde, Julie Krieckhaus as Chava, and Diana Gish in the role of the Rabbi. Mark Swezey was new to Vassar audiences in the role of Tevye, but in 1970, as a student at Ottawa University, he auditioned for the theatre's first season and was invited to come to Vassar at that time. A native of New York, he did give the offer some consideration but declined in favor of playing that particular summer season in New York City with Cafe La Mama!

Christopher was scheduled to help on *Fiddler*. As the show opened, he would be found perched up in the rafters above the stage, with a spotlight focused on him. With Kate's practice violin in hand, he would pretend to fiddle as the *Fiddler's* theme would arise from the prelude. This was not the first show Chris had worked from the rafters. In 1976, during *Oklahoma*, like everyone, he had multiple duties, one of which was to climb into the rafters to drop down Laurie's veil during the ballet marriage sequence. One evening, with peanut butter sandwich and veil in hand, Chris began his climb. As he reached the top some fifteen feet above the stage, he lost his grip. Veda and Bruce happened to be sitting in the back of the house that evening. They heard the quiet "thump," and knew immediately what had occurred. When they reached their son backstage, he was already up, climbing back to the bridge above, this time <u>without</u> sandwich in hand.

Chris often had the job that no one else could do—he had a knack for doing things in full view of the audience without taking focus or being noticed. When something would accidentally fall from the stage, he could, during performance, squeeze into the audience from under the stage and get it without anyone seeing him. In 1972, during *The Two Orphans*, there was such an instance where a prop would often fly from the stage during performance to land at the feet of the front row patrons who were already almost sitting on stage. Just before intermission Chris would retrieve the object and unobtrusively set it back for use later in the show. One evening, a front row audience member, who enjoyed playing practical jokes, picked up the prop and put it in his pocket. When Chris went to get it, the affable jokester had a good laugh.

Veda played for the rehearsals of *Dames*, but an accompanist had been hired for *Fiddler*. The pianist did not arrive until June 2, which was only four days to curtain. She rehearsed with the cast for two days, and then simply walked out! Two days before opening!

During the audition process, Bruce would always apologize for whatever pay he would be offering a prospective company member. He would tell them, "No matter how little you may be paid, I assure you it is by far more than I get!" That was all too true, for although some summers might prove to have large audiences, they never garnered much profit. The rural community where the theater was located was not very prosperous. The nightly car count found that most of the audience came from Osage, Franklin and Shawnee counties. Of the three, Shawnee County, Topeka's location, about 30 miles away, was the most prosperous. Still, the owners believed they had to keep the ticket prices at an affordable range, whatever that was, and they were satisfied when a summer broke even. This did not mean, however, that profit was impossible. It so happened that the two seasons prior to 1978 had shown fairly nice profits and that kept their hope alive.

When a player agreed to join the company, he or she was offered a contract, which had been prepared at first, by the partners' lawyer and, later, amended as the years passed to cover the addition of the Whippoorwill duties and other changes that might have occurred within the regular summer schedule. Each player, under contract, was offered a place to stay and three meals daily, which required each person to also assist the cook in the meal preparation. K.P. It was often dreaded, but the players never refused their duty when it came time for their KP shift.

When the piano player walked, there were certain rights the owners could utilize under her contract, but those rights were not exercised. Bruce always felt it wasn't worth the turmoil and expense of pursuing recourse under the contract. And, in this particular case, for it was very seldom that they had a player leave a season early, Veda had already made the tape for the boat show and that cast didn't need her piano services at the moment. And, with two days to go, it was decided for her to step in and accompany *Fiddler*. Both shows were set to open that week, *Fiddler* on the 6th of June, and *Dames* on the 8th. It was also a noisy tech week, for although the construction of the barn expansion to enclose the shop and add the patio was basically complete, rehearsal was frequently interrupted with roofers banging away.

When Bruce was not at the boat helping to get it painted and the valves installed for the summer cruises, he was on his knees laying a brick patio on the south and east sides of the barn. Carole Lynes stopped in on the first of June and provided a lot of help. John's firm in Wichita had long since been acquired by Cargill and he and his family had been moved to the firm's Minneapolis headquarters. She and son, Scott, were at that time on their way to Wichita to visit family for a few days. She had laid a brick patio at a former residence and her expertise was just what the bricklaying project needed. Together, she and Bruce prepared the bed by leveling a thick layer of sand inside the forms, which Bruce had already installed. She showed him how to lay a two by four on the sand and work it little by little until the carpenter's level, which had been placed on top of the board, would show that area to be even. After laying several courses, he felt confident that he could finish with some more hands.

"Okay, if you're not in a scene, you can come out here and lay some of these bricks!" Bruce put in a call for help.

Dames at Sea 1978. Back L-R: Larry Pressgrove, Tom Mitchell and David Ollington. Front L-R: Maggie, Linda Waltz and Kate.

On Tuesday morning, photos of *Dames* were taken and printed. One of the season newcomers, Brad Johnson, was a photographer who would become a godsend to Veda for that task. The morning also held a rehearsal for *Fiddler*. The day was high with excitement. Opening night. The carpenters were still not quite through with the roof, but at least, they would not be hammering during performance. By shortly after noon, Bruce had finished the bricklaying, and chairs and tables were set around for the customers to enjoy their pre-show entertainment and intermission dessert. The pre-show was usually planned, but those rehearsals were never as intense as for the primary performance. Pre-show was used as an opportunity for the players to warm up. They would sing familiar songs, usually somewhat in keeping with the evening show, but not songs from that show, and then, they would greet the audience and have a chance to also warm them up for the evening entertainment. Sometimes the costumes for the pre-show were the same as for the rest of the evening. Other times the players were dressed in their street wear for the pre-show. It was relaxed and the customers often looked forward to the pre-show as much as they did the feature presentation.

One of company perquisites of a season at Vassar was a test dinner and show aboard the boat, and the *Dames* cast were ready to try their show out on the *Fiddler* cast. On Wednesday evening, following the performance at the barn, the "Barnies," as the boat personnel called the players in the barn shows, were treated to a late dinner cruise and performance of *Dames*. What a fun and zany piece that show is and the cast really needed the audience so as to determine where the laughs would occur. Of course, an audience of your peers is not exactly the same as a regular audience, but it was a test, and everyone passed. It was the owners' belief that a boat show began when the passenger came aboard the Whippoorwill with the presentation of the food being as important as that of the show. Thus, the stewards were trained in how to carry the plates, how to set them before the customer and how to keep from drawing focus, if they had to perform a task while the show was in progress. Getting the food to the table was often a challenge, for the server had to keep the plates level as the boat might be listing in a turn or in the wake of a passing motorboat. The breeze, too, was unpredictable. It was not uncommon for salad to blow off the plate as the steward was taking up the first course. The insects could also present themselves for a taste, which would mean scrapping that plate and getting a new one. Catering the boat meant calculating food for the number of reservations, plus hoping that they had allowed for all of the above variances.

The steam engines on the boat had their own personalities, as well, and it was sometimes a struggle harnessing the steam for the warming table, to keep appropriate temperature for the food.

"Don't allow the food to cook—just enough steam to maintain serving temperature."

An evening on the boat was scheduled to fill a full four-hour evening, from casting off to landing. The pilot would try to vary the path of the cruise, depending upon the weather and the sunset. Usually, if the sun were bright, the boat would begin a westward direction, so that the customers were not blinded by its evening glow. If cloudy, the boat might head north up Wolf Creek or east towards the area of the dam. It all depended on the weather, the wind and the amount of traffic on the lake.

Bernie was not only new to piloting, but also, he was unfamiliar with Pomona Lake, so the first diversions in direction were new adventures for him. Learning the proper timing was the most important part of his job. It would take several seconds from the turn of the pilot wheel to a responsive reaction from the boat, and this was impossible to learn without actually steering a cruise. The different channels leading into the lake brought different currents and, depending on the level of the lake and with practice, the one steering the boat would learn to recognize and deal with those changing currents to keep the cruise at a relaxed and even pace. The passengers enjoyed the slow pace and sound of the Whippoorwill's paddle wheel as it lazily propelled the boat around the lake. One such regular customer and his wife, who were season ticket holders both at the barn and the boat, remarked one night to Bruce that they had traveled around the world and been on some excellent cruises, but that they found no evening more pleasant than one on Pomona Lake's own Whippoorwill Showboat.

Another evening during an earlier season, that particular couple had arrived for their night on the boat, an evening the boat was "over sold," and a table had been placed just before the pilothouse for them. Over sold? Well, no one was ever able to determine just what the capacity of the steamboat was. There were seventy-five or eighty life jackets aboard, but to give enough room at their tables for the passengers, and to leave room for them to walk around the deck, a load of fifty passengers was considered a full ship.

When the couple in question was shown to their private table reserved in front of the pilot's cabin on the second deck, they became disgruntled and incensed that they didn't have their normal table close to the small stage at the stern of the ship. Veda, who happened to be in the show for that cruise, came on board just before casting off and some of the crew approached her saying,

"We've got an unhappy couple on board," and they proceeded to relate the cause.

Veda had grown to know that particular couple over the years and she pondered the situation as she mounted the stairs to the second deck. She greeted the customers who were sitting at tables on the upper deck and proceeded to the pilothouse, where she passed a few words to Greg Clevenger, who was steering the craft that summer. She then "noticed" the couple sitting at the front of the boat and exclaimed,

"Oh, you have my favorite spot! This is where Bruce and I like to sit when we take an evening on the Whippoorwill. It's very private and the view is not hampered by other passengers." She didn't give them opportunity for complaint and none was offered. At the end of the evening, as the couple was leaving the craft, they asked to have that spot reserved for them for the next show. It was the nicest evening they had ever had on the boat. Veda's "Candidean" philosophy? "Everything happens for the best!"

It was the pilot who was responsible for deciding which direction to sail and when to change course so that the boat would be settled down in a quiet place in time for the show. He would learn how to use the bells to signal the engineer to reverse direction, slow down or stop. The Whippoorwill was to mean a whole new education for Bernie, and Bruce planned to sail with him until he was thoroughly trained in his task.

Sunsets on the boat were a high point of the evening's presentation. After Greg Clevenger joined the crew in 1975 to pilot the boat for the next three summers, the cast and crew would thereafter rate the evening sunset on a scale of 1 to 10. It was a ritual they all anticipated and argued about.

"Look at those colors! Now, that has to be a 9.5."

"No, we had a better one last week. Remember last Thursday? Tonight's an 8."

In 1978 Greg had become an officer in the US Marine Corps and was, by that evening in June, somewhere in California in training to fly helicopters. Greg actually believed that steering the Whippoorwill had given him valuable experience for piloting an airplane. Compensating for current, whether by air or water, would be a common factor, supposedly, but the instruments on the Whippoorwill would vastly differ from those of a high tech helicopter.

Therefore, as the evening sunset would begin, it was the pilot's job to dock the boat where all could enjoy that natural display. This action would also signal the time for the cast to prepare for curtain. Usually, the boat would pull into shore for the evening show, but occasionally, if the lake were particularly calm, it might drop anchor in the middle. That was a rare occasion, however, because a slight breeze might blow the hat off an actor or cause a fluctuation in the current of steam pressuring the generator which provided electricity for the evening's performance. Any fluctuation would cause the tempo and pitch to vary. The mayflies were usually worse along shore, but that disadvantage was cast aside by the other perils of performance.

Even with cutting some time off at the beginning of the test cruise for the *Fiddler* cast, the late night dinner cruise did not end until 2:30 a.m. By the time the docking ritual was practiced and the cleanup was complete, the cast and crew were able to get to bed an hour later.

Everyone was allowed to sleep in on Thursday. A gorgeous day, the boat show had a beautiful opening cruise and the weather remained perfect for several days. Weather was always a concern even before adding the boat to their summer fare, because their nightly log proved that variations in the weather would have a comparative impact on the size of house. For instance, rainy weather would produce "no show" tickets left in the box office. Nor would there be many walk-up tickets sold on such an evening. Their tracking method included the number of reservations that were on the books prior to curtain and the number of walk-ins they had after 7:00 pm. They knew for a fact that the entertainment industry, at least in Vassar, Kansas, was tied to the weather. That was true even before they bought the boat. Now, with the boat, they felt even more dependent on the weather than before.

Shortly after they had married, Bruce was inducted into the US Air Force to become a navigator. His one year of training at the US Air Force Base in Harlingen, Texas, included the study of weather along with the navigation tools to use for keeping an airplane on its course. After graduating as a First Lieutenant in 1958, he and Veda, who was by then pregnant with their first daughter, Kathryn, moved to Plattsburgh, New York, where he joined a unit of the Strategic Air Command. SAC was as much a buzzword of the 60's as peace and love. Americans feared Russia. The president would talk of peace while simultaneously gearing up missile silos in out of the way rural places that might not be seen as target spots for the Commies. SAC was one of the military programs that came in after the Korean "Conflict," and Bruce spent almost two years watching the weather and recommending the direction of flight to compensate for the many unpredicted changes that the weather brought to a day's maneuvers.

On Tuesday the 13th of June, 1978, a group of senior citizens had chartered the boat for a noon dinner show and cruise. It was such a pretty day and the boat looked clean and colorful with its coat of fresh paint. Jim Olson reported that during the cruise one of the passengers stopped him to comment,

"You young people have made a lot of old people happy this afternoon!"

On Wednesday, June 14th, a wind came up. It was hot, dry and dusty. This weather continued for the next three days. What clouds they had were not particularly heavy, but the days were just unpleasantly windy and in the evenings, the wind, although slackening, would still persist. It didn't seem to impact the evening cruise, because Bruce would have Bernie stay pretty close to the south shore where the heavily wooded bank would shield that portion of the lake from the south breeze. Friday night's audience was a charter group, a gourmet club from Overland Park. To charter a regular performance night, the group had to buy out the boat—50 seats. This group had come by bus and the passengers were already feeling their sauce when they arrived. The cast said they were rude and very drunk. Although the players were up for the performance, it was not a pleasant evening at the boat.

Fiddler, on the other hand, rated a spontaneous standing ovation on Friday. Part of the daily routine would include periodic appearances before various television talk shows and civic club programs, anything to help get an audience. On Friday morning Jennifer and Mark and Veda had gone to Topeka to appear on the Noontime with Nancy Perry show, Channel 49. They sang "Do You Love Me?" and Jennifer, as the head cook for the season, demonstrated her art of making French bread. It was a very successful appearance and that must have spurred the leading actors toward the evening's performance which deserved the honest applause.

Mark Swezey as Tevye
Fiddler on the Roof 1978.

Chapter Seven

They had continued their search for a loan to fund the expansion project. How they were able to squeeze in time to meet with bankers is not remembered. But they did. By June the project at the barn was well underway. They had obtained a loan against the equity in their home from a Winfield bank and another small loan from the Lyndon Bank, which helped to finish paying for the addition on the barn and provided the funding to move the railroad cars onto the premises. The caboose and three passenger cars all came from Sedalia, Missouri. Having retired the passenger cars, they were supposedly unfit to be transported by rail. However, the Missouri Pacific Railway, or MOP, as it was commonly called, would bring them in unannounced and set them on a siding in Vassar. An official from the railway would then telephone the couple that their car had been delivered. Each day that a car sat on the siding meant money out of pocket, for once it was delivered, the railway charged a drayage fee for the idle car. It was a treat for Veda to discover one of her cars sitting in Vassar when she went to the post office or grocery.

"Bruce, the dining car arrived last night!" Sure enough, the phone would ring to announce that drayage had begun.

It was in their best interest to get the cars moved to the Playhouse as soon as possible, and a company had been hired to do the job. Three brothers, the Stadler Brothers, the company members called them. Red Stadler was the principal who oversaw the setting of the cars. He first began moving the boxcars, which came from Topeka, onto the premises. Once the freight cars were set, the next to be moved was the caboose, because it would sit on the south end of the railroad track. Following would be *Cendrillon*, the parlor car, *Le Clemenceau*, the diner and *Ocean View*, the kitchen car which would sit just west of the shop area behind the barn.

Because the playhouse was located so close to the tracks which were the main line of the Missouri Pacific, the cast was accustomed to the sounds of trains with their mighty locomotives and whistles blowing during performance. Veda remembered one evening while watching a performance of *Annie, Get Your Gun*, a train passed during a boisterous rendition of *I've Got the Sun in the Morning*, and the train could still be heard over the chorus. The noise from the trains usually did not adversely affect the performances, unless their passing occurred during a moment of pathos or at the punch line in a moment of comedy.

The track was located on the east end of their property and then curved to the west. Westbound trains passed through Ottawa, then Pomona, Lomax, Vassar and Osage City on their way to the Pacific, and there was a long hill between Lomax and Vassar. The grade was not so steep, but it was a steady uphill climb for about three miles and, if the train were heavily laden with freight or many cars, the interruption in a performance might last ten or fifteen minutes. One especially long interruption occurred during a presentation of *Mark Twain Tonight*, which was given in 1971 by a Winfield friend of Veda and Bruce, Stuart Mossman. He had been giving performances of Mark Twain's speeches and short stories for years and, by that summer, had become quite accustomed to his role. When a reporter once asked him how he compared his interpretation to that of the famous Hal Holbrook, he responded in a characteristic drawl,

"Mr. Holbrook gives a very good imitation of the man, but I *am* Mark Twain."

During his performance, as the train was making its way up the hill, Mossman decided to give it time by taking that moment to light a cigar. This act was a presentation in itself requiring a good five minutes. He would walk over to the chest which stored his stock of cigars, take one out, walk back to his chair, start to put the cigar in his mouth, and remember that he had forgotten to get a match. He would then shuffle back to the bureau to get a match, amble downstage, look out at the audience as if just seeing them for the first time, begin to say something, think better of it and lift the cigar to his mouth. This business was choreographed and timed to perfection. The actor was able to improvise other business, which the audience would find amusing, but the business of lighting the cigar always drew applause.

With the train demanding such a great amount of time, and not wanting to shout over it, after lighting his cigar, he took a long draught, looked out at the audience, gestured to the passing freight caravan and said nonchalantly,

"Those things aren't even invented yet." An erroneous statement, perhaps, but the audience howled.

Red Stadler and his brothers became fixtures at Vassar Playhouse during the summer of 1978, because it took almost all summer for them to move the caboose, three passenger cars and three freight cars onto the corner to create Vassar Junction. A fourth passenger car, a Santa Fe compartment car named Regal Ruby was brought later onto the premises to become housing for the company of actors.

The players became very fond of the brothers. The Stadlers knew what they needed to do to get the job done, but they worked leisurely. Well, after all, summers are hot in Kansas, and these men weren't particularly young. They made their own hoisting equipment, fashioning the trailers for carrying the cars from their locations on the siding. They would first bring over the trucks, the wheels of the train. How many times one will wait at a crossing to watch a train pass and not realize the weight of those great wheels that bear the cars. The company learned lots of things that summer and the fact that each set of trucks weighs 10 ton is just one of the trivial facts picked up during the season.

Bruce and Veda had gotten together the money to purchase and set the cars, but they still needed funding for the renovation of their train into an attractive turn-of-the-century fine food establishment. They had taken their proposal to three or four banks and had been declined. Finally, at the suggestion of one banker, they made a trip to Kansas City to meet with the Small Business Loan Administration and make application for a direct loan. To be eligible for the program, a potential borrower had to be turned down by at least three banks. They met the criteria. The paperwork for their application arrived on Friday, June 16th, and Veda and Bruce worked on the application all day Saturday, in order to have it ready to mail after the weekend.

Chapter Eight

From Veda's diary, Saturday, June 17, 1978:

Tragedy. Tragedy. Such wind all day—just like preceding days. Bruce said last night the wind was to quit today. Sure enough, at 5:00 p.m. or thereabout, the wind did quit. And then, it was very pleasant.

I had worked on the loan application all day. We had a full house scheduled at barn, so I planned to dress early to help Eleanor in the box office. Around 7:15, Roger Aday cried, "Veda, come watch this funnel!"

Shortly, thereafter, a man drove up and said, "The Whippoorwill has capsized!"

Such a long night spent between checking passengers, crew and the morgue identifying bodies. We came home around 3:30 or 4:00 a.m. Rescue work had ended for the night to resume again early tomorrow. The count is now 8 dead and 7 missing. Tina is missing.

The storm seems to have originated right at the boat. So strange.

Larry P was trapped under (in the engine room) 45 minutes!

Chapter Nine

She clung to him as he sobbed.

"I should have died, too! I really wish I had."

"Please don't say that; you know how fortunate I feel that you are here with me, that you survived."

They had shared nearly forty years, twenty-two of which while married. She knew she had been lucky to have been with the same person for that long and to still find reason to remain. They had grown up together, gone through elementary school, high school, even college, together. They had worked together on so many projects, sometimes with differences, but none of which was ever irreconcilable. Apparently they loved being together. If that is love, then so be it. She was remembering a day in Junction City when she served as a substitute teacher for a high school class on marriage and family. She understood that the class fulfilled some state requirement of that time when schools had to offer a curriculum in health. The topic of that day's discussion was how to tell when it is true love. She had asked the question and several students responded with answers that seemed to stem more from sexual desire than anything else. Having been married only a few years at that time, she had to admit to the class that she did not know what real love was, but she felt it went beyond physical desire, as important as that might be in a relationship.

The couple was sitting at the doorway of a large room in the Corps of Engineers office that was located on the south edge of the dam. The room was in use as a morgue to receive the bodies that were being retrieved from the lake. She had remained with the coroner, Dr. Dwight Adams, from Osage City, all night. Dr. Dwight and his brother, Paul, another doctor, were very familiar to the players. When anything required medical services, they would see one of the Drs. Adams. Besides the medical attention, they were also prime supporters of the theater, being some of the first to purchase their season tickets each December. The owners had come to appreciate their attendance, not only for the applause they brought, but also, for their valuable comments pertaining to the season or the evening performance. They and their families were discerning theater patrons and they had the respect of the company of actors.

On this evening Dr. Paul was out of town; thus, Dr. Dwight had assumed the coroner's duties for the weekend. Armed with the list of missing passengers and information concerning them, Veda would identify the bodies as they were brought in and Dr. Dwight would examine them and tag them with the cause of death, *by drowning*. It was Monday morning before the last victim, a little girl, was found. The tally was initially 15 persons dead, but one of the young women was eight months pregnant, and the fetus brought the total to 16 persons dead.

"I know it would be much easier for you if you had perished; but just think how much worse you might be feeling right now if Kate or Maggie had drowned. You know how lucky I am that all three of you survived."

They spent that weekend between the banks of the lake watching the rescue operations, the Vassar State Park office, meeting with survivors and making their attempts at consolation, and the morgue, handing over the victims to their grieving spouses, parents and families. With each meeting all she could say was,

"I am so sorry."

Sorry, yes, that the event happened, but she had done nothing to deserve the events of June 17, 1978. Nor had anyone else. It was an act of God, that's how their lawyers would term it. An act of God.

The tornado, albeit small, arose from a waterspout. The time was about 7:10 pm. The boat had just left its dock and several passengers had remarked what a beautiful evening it would be. One, who would fall victim that evening, was a pilot who remarked to his friend, another pilot, just before casting off,

"This would be a great night for a flight, right?"

Bernie had pointed the bow west into the setting sun. Bruce was standing before the pilothouse when he noticed the small waterspout. He advised Bernie to turn back to shore and the pilot responded with a sharp turn of the pilot wheel. Before the boat had time to complete its turn and head into shore, the spout was on the starboard side, easing the craft over port. When it had accomplished that act, it rose into the air and hovered around the cove for a few minutes before it was joined by two other small funnels to create further havoc on the north shore before dissipating. Other property was damaged, but The Whippoorwill bore the only casualties in the tornado's path.

After the pickup carrying its messenger had left, Veda jumped into her car with several members of the *Fiddler* cast and drove to the lake. They could still see a couple of funnels over the cove and they first headed for the shore where the wharf boat was docked, because she was unsure whether the boat had yet cast off or not. There was a communication system between the barn and boat, but she hadn't stopped at the barn to ask if anyone from the boat had called. She had a husband and two children, not to mention her responsibility for all the passengers and crew, on that boat and she knew she had to get there fast and ease her fears. Little could she know what her worst fears would be.

When she and Bruce had made the decision to acquire the Whippoorwill, she went to their insurance agent to arrange for liability insurance. The first question he asked was,

"How much coverage do you want?"

"I have no idea. You know more about what is appropriate than I do."

"Well, then, tell me—what would a worst case scenario be?"

"Worst case? Well, I've heard stories of the boilers of steamboats exploding. I guess that would constitute worst case. I can't imagine that it would happen, but we should probably be prepared." And the agent wrote what he felt would be a policy sufficient for that hypothetical tragedy.

When the car arrived at the dock, a camper recognized her and, pointing to the south shore across the park, he said,

"The boat is over there. Everybody is okay. They're bringing them in to the marina."

She drove over to the south shore and, looking out upon the lake, she was horrified by what she saw. Something resembling a whale was offshore, approximately 100 yards maybe, with a few people on its back. She was stunned with the realization that she was seeing the bottom of the boat's hull. Unable to recognize any of the persons, she didn't have time to stare very long, for a pontoon was loading some of them to bring them back to shore. She and the cast members in her car went to the marina where she saw Kathryn, Margaret, Linda, Tom, Jim and some others of the cast. Her memory was blurred. She asked about her husband and was told that he was on the boat directing rescue operation. After they had come out of the water and were sitting on the hull, they had heard tapping in two different places and realized there must be some survivors who had found air pockets in the boiler and engine rooms. Tom and Linda told her that they were sure one of those persons was Larry Pressgrove. He had been working with Jim Olson in the little kitchen serving food from the steam table. Jim said that when the boat began to tip he left the kitchen with Larry still in it. He thought it was likely he could have made his way to the engine room.

There were also several other persons at the marina and she didn't know whether they were passengers or curious onlookers. As she was talking to the cast members hearing each of their stories, a man was brought to the marina. He was crying and when she approached, he reached hold of her arm saying,

"My wife was with me, do you know where she is?"

"I'm certain we will find her soon," was all she could say. She had learned that survivors were being taken to the park office and, as she had not been there, she was yet to realize the number of persons missing. It so happened that the man who inquired about his wife was one of the persons who had been trapped in an air pocket. He was rescued from the boiler room.

Meanwhile, Bruce was onsite. Lawrence Stadel, an experienced diver, had brought equipment to the boat to rescue the ones who were trapped inside. Although Lawrence was familiar with the layout of the Whippoorwill, Bruce explained just exactly where the two spots would be and any obstacles that Lawrence might encounter. He dived under water, descending to the depth of the first level as Bruce had described, and reached the boiler room where he found one man. He spoke to the man and gently, with his expertise, led him back the way he had come, guiding him to the lake's surface. Bruce again explained the layout and Lawrence returned to find the engine room to rescue Larry Pressgrove.

Larry first came to the Playhouse in 1976. He and Tom Mitchell had attended Shawnee Heights High School, where Veda's brother, Dick, taught math. Although Dick was no longer associated with the playhouse, he would continue to steer talent in that direction. And Larry and Tom, along with a third classmate, Scott Wible, were encouraged by him to apply to Vassar. They were all hired in one capacity or another and cast in the production of *Oklahoma*. The trio became a duo the next two years. Although Scott did not return as a permanent player, he did continue to attend many shows and also, to work a future season as the publicity and program designer. But Larry and Tom became entrenched at Vassar for several seasons.

During the summer of 1977, the company rallied to Larry's support when his younger brother was accidentally killed. It was a tragedy that brought everyone to his side. Although there was nothing anyone could do to assuage his grief, they were available for him to cry to, scream at or to serve as a punching bag, if he needed one. Everyone knows the adage "The show must go on," and it is true. Sometimes the theater, giving an actor the advantage of escape into another character for the period of a rehearsal or performance, helps one to work through the problems that life has cast upon his path. Although the company of 1977 knew the grief that Larry bore during the final weeks of the season, he continued to make the performances. His personal tragedy had brought him even closer to everyone who worked with him. On this night of tragedy, it was no surprise that there was much anxiety among the players who knew that Larry was among the list of missing persons. There was much celebration, and many prayers of gratitude were said, when he was rescued from the pit of the engine room.

The opening routine of the summer was always so hectic. You got to know your fellow company members by working with them, and, as the Whippoorwill had just embarked on the eighth cruise of the season, none of the players knew Tina Kramer so well as her classmate, Aaron Gragg, and her sister, Debbie. She was less than a year younger than Debbie and the sisters shared more than a family bond. They were also best friends. Tina was quiet, very pretty and always cooperative. She was one of the last players to help Bruce finish the brick laying for the patio at the barn. Tough work for tender hands, but Tina rolled up her sleeves and willingly put her fingers to those rough bricks, seeing that they were placed appropriately in each row, while maintaining an even and level height.

Veda had purchased a blue denim fabric to make special costumes for the stewards that year. They were sort of a sailor type, a one-size-could-fit-all shift for the girls and a shirt for the boys. The girls were all slender and the dresses becoming. Veda's last memory of Tina was seeing her run to catch a ride in the "banana wagon," the affectionate term given the company van. She noticed how pretty Tina looked in her steward's dress.

Tina's funeral was held in the biggest place that Quenemo had to offer, the high school gymnasium auditorium, and it was packed. Her family had lived in the community for at least two generations and there were many friends and family to fill the large room. Her parents, Willis and Ethel, asked Kathryn to sing for the services. Kate had been on the boat with Tina and, in spite of her own personal grief, the emotion of the hour and the memory of her fears during the storm itself, Kate's voice soared with clarity, beauty and compassion. Afterwards, Veda took her daughter in her arms saying,

"I was so proud of you." And Kate wept. Through her tears she cried,

"That was the hardest performance I have ever given in my life." Indeed, she was never to know another event so painful, but her mother would.

* * *

How do the media treat a tragedy? Like vultures, they sweep down pecking away at the victim's flesh until only a skeleton remains. That was another axiom learned by the company that summer. The Whippoorwill made local news, state and national news and world news. On the night of the tragedy, in the office of the Corps of Engineers, Veda and Bruce had overheard someone asking why this event was getting so much press, and a representative from UPI or AP stated,

"There just isn't anything else happening this weekend."

How sad. How cold. It is recognized that reporters have a job to do, but this "event" appeared to bring out tactics and maneuvers more befitting of journalistic war games. Each time any of the players stepped off the grounds, and even sometimes when the media personnel were encamped on the premises, they would be besieged by someone with a pencil or a microphone asking questions. Bruce and Veda cautioned the players to not answer the media only because they felt that the probing questions would upset them even more than they already were, and also, because news reports tend to be sensationalized whenever possible. God knows the tragedy of the Whippoorwill did not need to be blown out of proportion.

The irony was that, after eight years of summer theatre, here was the opportunity for the playhouse to take focus—the whole world is a stage—and that thought turned everyone's stomach. It was too painful to describe. The players did plenty of talking and recapping of the events among themselves; and they also had to put their thoughts and memories of the occurrence onto paper for the authorities, but no, they wanted the media out of their lives. It was not appropriate for the radio, television and newspapers to invade and take advantage of their pain. Especially, when the first question was, without exception,

"How did you feel?" Like crap, that's how. No—worse than that.

Over five years later, in 1983, when Veda and Bruce were on a two-week Eurorail trip through France and Germany, on two different occasions they were visiting with someone, each a native of the land—thank goodness, most speak English, as Veda's flimsy French and fractured Deutsch are not sufficient for easy conversation—and the dialogue would turn to where they had come from.

"Kansas? I remember reading about a boat—" Not *Oz*, rather, their own fifteen minutes of fame, and they couldn't even enjoy it.

At breakfast on the Sunday morning following the storm, Bruce noticed Jan Feager sitting at the table. She had come in during the afternoon.

"You!" He pointed at her. "You were on the boat! I remember seeing you in the water!" He said he had not reported Jan's name as one of the passengers or crew. A former player from the season of 1975, she was then living and working in Kansas City and often made a trip to spend the weekend with her friends at Vassar. Bruce was remembering the times during the season of 1975 when Jan would spend evenings after a show tapping the night away with a fellow hoofer, Mark Harryman. Mark and she had performed together the first season for Worlds of Fun in Kansas City. He was not only her friend, he was also the nephew of Veda's sister-in-law, Barbara, who lived nearby and whom Mark would come to visit when he was in the area. After leaving Worlds of Fun, he went on to dance professionally and tour with several personalities and professional Broadway tours. When he would visit, Jan and Mark would don their tap shoes and create their own music and rhythm, the sound of which would reverberate from the stage through the wee hours of the morning.

Bruce winced at the possibility of Jan being among the missing and him not even remembering she was there. He then recollected their going to the cliff together to check the weather at 6:30 p.m. before leaving for the boat. Checking the weather was one of Bruce's daily rituals. If there were what looked like storm clouds in the west, he would place a call to the weather bureau to see what the predictions were. If the weather were questionable, he then would make decision as to whether to cancel the cruise or what. Sometimes, they would stay tied to the dock for serving the meal and, if the weather cleared, they would cast off and complete the evening. If rain ensued, the policy was to make a refund if the evening was cancelled prior to completing dinner. On that evening, their view from the cliff revealed clearing in the west with partial clouds above and Jan had decided to take the cruise and see *Dames*.

Eleanor was in charge of answering the telephones and she was perfect for that task. She possesses a quick wit with a kind response and the ability to end an unwanted conversation without the person on the other end realizing that he has been cut off. As faithful as she was to the phone, she missed one call that came in for Larry. He was asleep and whoever answered that call awakened him to take it. Evidently the person on the other end had given indication that he was one of Larry's family. At least, the answering player felt it appropriate to wake him and when he took the phone, the sleepy young man was attacked by a reporter from *The Enquirer* or some such tabloid publication with a barrage of questions. Larry gave honest answers that were turned around and blown up resulting in several comments that were quite untrue in their published story. Other players were hit upon, and especially Veda and Bruce, but this instance was apparently the only one that was not averted. The players would watch the newscasts and the newspaper clippings were saved, usually without reading, so that they might be reviewed at a later time when one had more perspective.

"Where were you when the storm hit?" her father asked Margaret.

"I was on the starboard railing letting down an awning. The boat tipped over and I ended up swimming entirely under it before coming up again. I thought I would never surface!"

"I was on the lower deck at the bow and, when it began to tip, I literally walked off the starboard side into the water," Kathryn said.

Aaron also said he had seen the storm coming and just walked off the boat. One by one they would remember and recite their thoughts and experiences. It all had happened so suddenly, the horror of the event was impossible to fully describe. Once the boat was overturned, people began to surface. Some needed help and had to be pulled out of the water onto the hull. Bruce pulled out one passenger, an older man who was having difficulty breathing, and another passenger administered CPR. He tried to account for all of his crew; and he realized as he scanned the faces of the survivors that some were missing. All of them remembered passengers asking about other persons who had come on board with them. And then, they would tell of the tapping and the moment of realization that some persons were alive inside—the anxiety of reality and the fear of the unknown.

Chapter Ten

The news of the Whippoorwill, which was spread around the world, brought an out-pouring of love. Friends, strangers, so many persons reached out to see if they could help. One man from Wichita drove up and said, "I'm a carpenter. You don't have to pay me. I am just here to help." And he stayed and helped. It was several days before the boat was righted and emptied of water. But when it was floating again at its own dock, there were many repairs to be made. The storm did not wreak physical damage to the boat. No, that was caused by the rescue operations. To bring the boat up, the movers at the playhouse, the Stadler Brothers, used their hoists and cranes to drag the craft to shore. There was so much weight with the waterlogged craft, that when it was turned upright, it had a very prominent starboard list. Several thought it was hung up on a ledge. There were days with "Experts" trying to right the boat. Bill Hurtig, who had designed and built the craft, was present, but did anyone ask him how to raise it? Veda and Bruce were often present. They, too, had raised the boat several times when it had taken on water due to various reasons, one time was when the lake froze and the pressure of the ice pushed the hull under on the port side. The list at that time was similar to the present situation, but did anyone think Bruce might know how to bring it up? No. Bruce sat on shore with the Rev. Hurtig and they passed comments between them.

"They're going about it all wrong."

"I know. If they would pump the water from the starboard bilge into the port side, I think it would come right up."

They sat and chuckled at the frustrating efforts of the well-meaning experts who would not listen to either's suggestions. Finally, the "professionals" left probably thinking that they would let the boat sink where it was, once and for all. When they were gone by the following week, Bill brought in his brother, Armand, and Pop, his father, who got a pump and brought the boat up. It was exactly as they had discussed. They pumped the water from the sunken side into the side that was floating. The added weight to the high side created a balance to level the craft and lift up the starboard side. The simple science of balance and equilibrium.

At the Playhouse there was much discussion as to *when* the boat would be ready to resume sailing and very little question of *if* it would sail. When a man from Omaha showed up offering to purchase the craft, Bruce considered it for a while and decided he should ask the family. He first sought out Christopher, who responded,

"No way! We're not going to give up."

The other family and company members voiced the same sentiments, and Bruce didn't consider the possible sale any further. Declining the man's offer without even asking him the amount of his offer, he proceeded with planning the remaining season for the boat.

Eleanor was given the job of contacting the persons who had booked passage on the boat during the weeks it would be idle. She would arrange either the rescheduling or making of refunds. She also saw that letters of condolence were written to all of the survivors with their refund for the evening, which had ended before the dinner was served. Contributions, many of which were anonymous, began arriving from all parts of the country, and a fund was set up at the Lyndon State Bank. By the time Veda and Bruce learned of the fund, there had been collected some $10,000 to be used for the Whippoorwill. That fund was utilized to put the boat back into service for the summer. The goodness of strangers!

Meanwhile, Veda kept contact with the loan officer at the SBA to see if the couple would still be considered for a loan since the Whippoorwill tragedy. She was assured that the event would not impact their decision, because the SBA was not taking that craft as collateral anyway. She was asked to answer a few questions and then, make appointment to see the officer in two weeks. The ensuing time was spent with meetings; there was one to include the park and lake officials, the county sheriff's department, the insurance agent, Bill Hurtig and several attorneys. In addition, a representative from the National Transportation and Safety Board had come into the area to inspect the boat and interview the survivors. Many days were spent answering questions; all of the players were interrogated, whether they were on the boat or not. It felt like an extended exam.

"When do I learn if I passed or not?"

The initial incentive for having purchased the new chairs and gleaming paint job for the boat prior to the season opening had been the special hosting of the Kansas Tourism Task Force, which was set for June 21st. Carole Lynes drove up on the 20th with young son Scott in tow wanting to be of use. Such friendship. She and Veda motored to Ottawa to purchase fabric and then, Carole sewed new tablecloths to be used first, for the special dinner, and later, for when the boat would resume sailing. The *Dames* cast did not have a stage, but they banded together to prepare the food and the members of the task force who arrived that evening were treated to a meal on the new patio with *Fiddler* in the barn. The evening was first planned to include park and lake officials, but there was still so much activity with the Saturday's tragic incident, that the number of special guests was small.

Two weeks later Bruce and Veda made the trip to Kansas City to meet with the SBA and to purchase yet another supply of chairs and dishes for the boat. So much had been lost to the lake. The chairs that were rescued were not usable and dishes and steam pans simply sank to the lake's floor. Some of the players spent a few hours in diving and retrieved some of the equipment, but very little was salvaged. Upon their return from Kansas City, there was much curiosity from the players.

"Did you get the loan?" And Bruce responded,

"We were able to buy a supply of folding chairs. They'll be delivered in time for the next cruise."

"But what about your loan?"

"Well, I have good news and bad news."

"What's the bad news?"

"We had a flat tire." And there was whooping and hollering among the players.

The next scheduled show for the boat had been the revue of the music of Bruce's father, John L. Rogers. In the turmoil of recent weeks, however, Veda arranged for one of the players to take over and, instead of John L's music, prepare a revue of the music of Richard Rodgers, no relation. The new title was *Ring around Rodgers (with a "d")*. David Ollington, who was playing Motel in *Fiddler*, offered to direct the show and was gratefully accepted for the task. Using players who were not in the next barn production of *East Lynne*, he put together an energetic show for a two-week run. The season on the boat was further changed, because the Rogers show was to have been a split run with two weeks in July and a week during the middle of August. With its cancellation and with the *Dames* cast doing special road presentations in the area, another change was made. The slot on the boat titled *Follies* for which Veda was to have put together another revue—Stephen Sondheim songs—was changed to a run of the musical *Mack and Mabel*, with Mark Swezey as director.

The couple then invited Rick and Sally to come perform their own pastiche of Cole Porter songs to fill the *Rogers* August week. They agreed. The young couple was working at the ESU Summer Theater in Emporia that season, and it would close the end of July, so the timing was right. Rick was very fond of the Whippoorwill, having directed and acted in many shows for the boat, including its first dinner show voyage with *HMS Pinafore*. He had lots of stories and relished their telling, sometimes to the chagrin of the owners. For example, the boat had a small toilet with a sink which held a faucet that spurted lake water and where one could wash hands following a "pause for relief," but there was no stool. A portable toilet filled that need, and one of the evening assignments was to fill the "Port-a-Potty's" tank with water before each cruise, and then, at the end of the evening, empty the container at the park's waste station and wash everything thoroughly for the next day's use. When the couple first purchased the boat in 1974, Rick was hired to oversee its entire operation, including the dinner, the show, and the customers' comfort. Within a few weeks he was able to spout statistics on how many flushes you could get from "Sylvia" and the measures to take when she was full. The pot was named after the role of Sylvia Potter-Porter in *Annie, Get Your Gun*! Rick could make even the most menial chores seem a lark.

Rick first came to Vassar in 1973 to design and construct the set for *Hello, Dolly*. Like everyone he wore many hats. He was also chosen to play the role of Cornelius. A season at Vassar was, if nothing else, terrific preparation for the real world, including, but certainly not limited to, theater. The actors may have thought they would come to Vassar to become "a star," but when they left, they would possess a thorough knowledge for putting a show together. The KP and cook shifts for the boat, as well as the close living quarters, also prepared them for survival and life itself. Working together, shouldering their load, everything helped them toward becoming a whole person with an emphasis on theater.

In 1973, Rick arrived at the playhouse before the troupe, so as to begin construction on the set for *Hello Dolly*. His design included a ramp, which extended from the stage right balcony to a four by eight foot platform that he was erecting down stage right. Veda was already at the theater, as she typically made the move early in the season in order to get the place open, clean the quarters after the winter vermin had done their work, and begin work on publicity for the coming summer. It was a quiet time, that period in late spring, and she always looked forward to it in spite of knowing how much dirty work was ahead of her. One afternoon while logging the day's season ticket orders, she heard a great crash come from the barn. She ran to investigate and found Rick lying prone on the cement slab where the orchestra usually sat off stage right. He was dazed, but alive, under a large platform.

"What on earth were you doing?" she asked as she pried the heavy piece off and helped pull him from under it.

"I was installing the ramp."

The ramp was at least ten feet long and surely weighed seventy-five pounds. And, it was to be installed ten feet above the audience! "How could you even think of doing that by yourself?" Suffice to say, Rick rested the remainder of that day. On the next day, with some help from another player who had arrived, he got the ramp installed. The audience never knew the potential calamity as they watched the actors run back and forth between the balcony and the stage during that production.

Rick also designed the season's production of *The Lion in Winter*. He had the help of Bill Christie, another newcomer of 1973. Veda and Bruce knew Bill from seeing him in productions at Southwestern where he was a student. After playing Rudy in *Dolly*, he displayed his versatility by "weaving" the set for *Lion*. Using large pieces of burlap, he fringed and tied and somehow created a macramé setting befitting of England's King Henry II and his exiled wife Eleanor. The cleanup crew after rehearsals for that show would each day find a huge glob of lint under the seat where Bill had been working!

* 𝒥𝓊𝓁𝓎 5 - 2015 *

Each year brought some new faces to the stage. They would work a season and sometimes come back for more. It was always a pleasure to have players return who already had a feel for the place and what would be expected. But, it was also refreshing to have new players arrive. One such arrival was Mac Williams in 1971. Having worked with Ken Harden, who played the "villain" roles during Vassar's first season, at the Dallas Theater

Center, Mac came to Vassar expecting something far different from what he found. First of all, Ken had told him the place was located on a lake! Mac drove in with a friend, who was to stay a few days with him at the motel before taking herself back home to Texas, and found weeds, high weeds, lining the driveway. He looked toward the lagoon, in the east milo field, and wondered if that were the lake Ken had described. Upon hearing the description he had envisioned a theatre with a sweeping veranda and a large green lawn that swooped down to the banks of a beautiful lake. The placed looked dreary and Mac came very close to turning around and going back to Dallas. His friend encouraged him,

"Give it a try, Mac. They seem like nice people. You might enjoy it."

Okay, he would stay. Mac was cast in some pretty good roles for the summer, the young male lead, generally, and that was incentive enough for him to give it a go.

One of the plays set for that year was *Francesca da Rimini*, based on the Dante tale of two lovers. The script by nineteenth century playwright, Frances Boker, had been adapted especially for Vassar by Ken Harden, who would also be playing the role of the tragic Lanciotto whose love for Francesca is unrequited. In a jealous rage he kills the young lovers, Francesca and Paolo, at the end of the play. The supporting cast made the play just the right size for Vassar. Ken also adapted it to fewer sets than the original script required and the company was looking forward to that piece.

A week before going into rehearsals for *Francesca* they were playing Neil Simon's comedy, *Barefoot in the Park*, in which Ken was cast as Mr. Velasco, the older bachelor who lives upstairs. Veda was playing the opposite role of Mrs. Banks, the ingénue's mother, and Mac and Rosemary Luthi were cast as the newlyweds. They had also been set to play the young lovers in *Francesca*. During the run of *Barefoot*, Veda noticed that Ken became more and more morose as the first week was ending. He was working on the *Francesca* script at night after playing the performance and she and Bruce began to think something was wrong.

One early Sunday morning, following the first week of the *Barefoot* run, Veda noticed Ken pacing in the parking lot. Up and down—back and forth. Finally, he came over to the trailer where the family lived and knocked on the door asking to see Bruce, who was still sleeping. Veda woke her husband who dressed and went outside.

"What's the matter, Ken?"

Ken wanted to go for a drive. Veda watched as he got into the driver's side of their family car while Bruce slipped into the passenger side. The car went wheeling out of the parking lot and headed east. Bruce later told her that, in a ride so fast that he really feared for his life, they sped to the dam.

"I thought for awhile that Ken meant to drive into the lake!"

Ken was ill. He told Bruce he had been suffering from colitis all through the spring prior to that season and had spent some time in the hospital. As a student at Washburn University, he had dated Rosemary Luthi. Although she felt very close to him, her feelings toward him were platonic. It was believed that Ken had hoped a different relationship between them would develop that summer. His actions of the previous week were taken by the cast to be signs of jealous rage. In reality, he was physically ill from the colitis and insufficient sleep.

Bruce excused Ken from finishing the season and telephoned his parents in Topeka to come pick him up after that evening's show. After the performance and Ken's departure that night, the remaining cast members retreated to the rock house kitchen and held a *wake*.

Roger Cummings, who had also been a member of the company's first season in 1970, had that morning purchased a watermelon which was generously spiked with gin or vodka, allowing it to "marinate" all day. That evening he sliced the watermelon and everyone sat around the kitchen table eating the flavor-enhanced fruit and sharing memories of Ken Harden. Seated around the long table in the rock house were Mac, Rosemary, Roger, Sandy Eddings, Misty Maynard, John Friesen, David Polson, Jerry Smith, Bruce and Veda. The evening was quite therapeutic and all of the players were able to sleep in the next day, for Mondays were off!

In 1971 Tuesdays were also dark. On this particular week, Bruce and Veda had to go to Winfield to take care of some business and, during their six-hour round trip, they discussed what to do for the remainder of the season. They didn't feel it would be appropriate to continue with the Boker tragedy. During the drive, they made the decision to move *A Thousand Clowns*, which was then scheduled for the final slot of the season, up three weeks into the *Francesca* run, scrap the Boker tragedy and end the season with *Rashomon*. *Barefoot* still had two weeks on its run and Stuart Mossman was contracted to do a week of *Mark Twain Tonight* after the current show's run. They could do it.

The summer of 1971 was a season of "artistic success," but no profit. It started with Veda and Bruce doing the musical, *I Do! I Do!* by Tom Jones and Harvey Schmidt. The show had an earlier than usual opening, because the accompanist, Veda's nephew, John Friesen, was living at the couple's home in Winfield, while he attended Southwestern College. Having him so convenient, the pair began rehearsals in early May and were able to open the show the first of June. The crowds were slim, but the run did pick up. One night, however, Bruce and Veda looked out to see only three persons in the audience. It began raining as the curtain went up. After intermission, they again looked out, couldn't see their audience and thought they had gone home. Continuing on with the show, they learned later that their "audience" had moved under the balcony out of the rain! During their bows, the entire audience gave the duo a standing ovation!

Barefoot in the Park was the next show for three weeks and it sold pretty well. Following that was the one-man presentation of *Mark Twain Tonight* by Stuart Mossman. He drew commendably as did *A Thousand Clowns* which followed. For *Rashomon,* Bruce brought in a KU professor of Japanese theater, Andrew Tsubaki, to choreograph the fights. The play calls for several fights between the young husband, a Samurai Warrior (Mac Williams), and a bandit (Jim Reynolds). Each fight is described by a different witness to the scene, so the stories change as well as the fights. It is an interesting script and the set by Roger Cummings was very beautiful. Prof. Tsubaki provided invaluable help with the costumes as well as the action, and many years later he would tell the couple that their production was the first of what would be six different productions of *Rashomon* that he would be able to add to his artistic resume.

While attending school in Winfield, John Friesen had become a friend of one of Bruce's former high school students, Tom Grove, who had grown up in Winfield and who, like John, attended Southwestern College. As that spring ended, the two friends said goodbye and Tom went to California, John to Vassar. One evening, following her performance of Agnes in *I Do! I Do!*, Veda was confronted by John backstage with,

"I have terrible news."

The phone call, which everyone had heard during the evening's performance, was his friend, Jane Stinnett, another Winfield student who had been at Vassar the first season and was to return in 1972. She had called to tell them that Tom had been shot and killed in a robbery while working as a night clerk in a 7-Eleven Store in California. Veda was touched that her nephew would spare her such grief until the evening show was over. In fact, she didn't really cry until the following day when she wrote a long tear-stained letter to the grieving parents in Winfield.

The Herb Gardner comedy, *A Thousand Clowns*, calls for a ten-year old boy. Chris was ten, but he didn't seem suited for the role. With a slight frame and quick movement, he seemed more suited to comic roles. The role of Nick was for a serious and precocious young boy. Bruce asked Kate to read for the part and she won the role. Kate was twelve at the time, short for her age, somewhat chunky and wore glasses. Her mother gave her a boy's crop and her name in the program was simply "K. Rogers." Very few audience members realized she was a girl. Jim Reynolds, who had been a reviewer for the Topeka Capital Journal, was brought in to play the role of the TV clown. Mac and Rosie played the leads and Roger Cummings was selected to play the brother, Arnie. Roger had difficulty identifying with the role of Arnie. A child of the 60's and an art student at Lindsborg, Roger wore his hair long and the role was going to mean a conventional haircut. He rehearsed the show for a week and then, without telling anyone, he disappeared. Not knowing for sure what to do, Bruce decided to step into the role. After another week, Roger returned. He apologized. He didn't wish to leave Vassar, but he said he could not play that role. Bruce assured him it was okay. Then, in the final show *Rashomon*, Roger was cast as—guess? The priest! He shaved his long hair for that role! The players had a ceremony to perform the rite and Sandy Eddings and David Polson held the honored roles of "Executioners."

Mac Williams also brought another skill to Vassar. On the evening of July 4th, he taught the players how to build hot air balloons. Now, please do not tell anyone you read this here! They took a large plastic bag such as you get from the local cleaners, placed some drinking straws to form a cross and tied the straws to the bag. They then melted wax to hold many small birthday candles along the straws. Finally, they lit the candles and watched the bag (balloon) fill with warm air until it began to lift and float off into the night sky. It was really a beautiful sight to see. Before the evening was over, neighboring residents in the area were telephoning the authorities with reports of UFO's. In addition, they heard the next day that one of the balloons, with candles still afire, had landed in a nearby field igniting some dry wheat stubble left from the summer's harvest. Thankfully, it didn't burn long and no harm was done.

CHAPTER ELEVEN

The Christmas of 1969, after Bruce and Veda had informed their Winfield friends of plans to start a theater at Pomona Lake, cans of barn red paint began appearing on their front porch. By the end of that holiday season, they had collected enough paint to cover the barn. What a joyous gift! They asked several persons who the responsible person was, but that remained a secret. They could only guess the idea probably originated with their good friends, Wayne and Jane Cherveny. Wayne had been cast as Sky Masterson in the first Winfield Community Theatre 1967 production of *Guys and Dolls*, and in the following summer of 1968, Jane served as co-director with Veda for the WCT children's production of *The Wizard of Oz*.

The auditions for the first children's theater event in many years brought out over 140 kids ranging in ages six through seventeen to sing and dance for a spot in *The Wizard of Oz*. Veda and Jane heard all of them sing their piece and then, met for the purpose of casting. After choosing the persons to fill the speaking roles and much further discussion, they realized they could not eliminate one single child. They announced the cast, set the schedule, met with the parents to explain the necessity of getting their child to each practice that called for them and they then began the rehearsal process.

Veda spent evenings blocking the Munchkins and other chorus numbers. She worked it so as to try to not have more than thirty or forty children on stage at one time. It was, after all, a small stage. What are we saying? There was no stage! The theater board had that spring of 1968 voted to do construction on the fairgrounds barn to provide additional seating and add a backstage area for their permanent theater space. Thus, when *Wizard* went into rehearsals, the barn was still under construction. Rehearsals were set for the high school gymnasium and other available spots as needed. Two to three weeks into rehearsal, they were able to move to the barn—but not to the stage. They had to rehearse in the loft above the new seating that had been installed. Veda and Jane were to laugh for a long time afterwards about rehearsing with scaffolding on stage!

There were many practices held in the loft where the orchestra would later sit. Veda would place the children and then, point to the stage to show them where their position would be when they got on stage. They would rehearse their entrances, songs and dances. Finally, the last week of rehearsal, the scaffolding came down, and the children were sitting in the new seats with Veda giving them their notes and directions when she said, "All right! Places! We will begin rehearsal now." The children all ran up the steps to the loft!

Working in the theater can be a strain on a relationship. Emotions are high and tempers close to the surface. Bruce was also involved in *Wizard*, as he helped to oversee the construction of the barn renovation and installation of the new lighting. The final week of rehearsal found him sweating in the new light booth where he and others were running cable and setting instruments. On the evening of the final dress rehearsal, when they still had no lights with which to practice, Veda was getting ready for a long, grueling evening as she was trying to decide whether she should take the time to take her children, who were of course in the show, for a sandwich, or whether she could ask Bruce to do it. With caution and what she felt was politeness, she approached Bruce who was working in the loft at one of the instruments,

"How are you coming?" There was no answer.

"Are you getting about finished?" There was again no answer.

"Do you want me to bring you some supper?" The third time no response.

"Are we going to have lights tonight?"

"HOW IN HELL DO I KNOW IF WE ARE GOING TO HAVE LIGHTS TONIGHT?" She always would regret that she was never able to exhibit *her* artistic temperament except within the framework of an onstage character.

* * *

The gift of some seventeen gallons of paint seemed like a stunt Wayne and Jane had probably arranged, and Bruce and Veda tried to think of some way to repay their Winfield friends. The winter of 1969-70 before their opening season passed so quickly what with meetings of the partners, creating signs, programs, publicity materials, planning the season and setting up auditions. While Bruce and Veda concentrated on that area of the theater, Ruth and Dick were busy with physical plans, hiring contractors to turn a hay barn into a theater. Plumbing the rock house, the barn and making additional runs for future buildings, mowing the weeds.

Bruce had planned that his Thanksgiving break of 1969 would be used to take down the Bretton Hotel tin ceiling that his wife had so admired during the Labor Day auction. He had received a call from Leonard that demolition was ready to include the first floor and the ceiling needed to come down if he was going to get it. He borrowed one of Leonard's twelve-foot stepladders and set off for the hotel with a thermos of hot coffee. The temperatures had dropped that week to somewhere in the 30's. There was much debris that kept falling as he worked to remove each piece carefully to keep from breaking the fragile and somewhat rusty tin. Finally, after several shivering hours and much persistence, he was able to get enough whole pieces to cover his own dining room ceiling. He gathered up the sculptured pieces of tin and went home.

In the meantime, Veda had taken a call from her brother, Dick, who was also using his Thanksgiving break from teaching to work and who needed some help at the Vassar barn. Upon returning home from his bitterly cold day in the debris of the Bretton, Bruce returned Dick's call to learn that while removing the hayloft to ready the barn for construction, the north end began to fall away. The hayloft was what had been holding the barn together! He had temporarily propped it up, but needed more hands to give it a measure of permanence. Bruce asked Wayne if he would like to help and sure, they met Dick at the soon-to-be theater the following morning. They found the north end of the barn bowed out about four feet. They nailed together some 2"x 6" timbers, pushed them into the ground at the side of the barn and pushed the north end back into place. It was sufficient to stabilize the barn until construction could begin the following spring.

By spring of 1970, Bruce and Veda had decided to hold a "paint-in" and invite their WCT friends to help. They conferred with Ruth and Dick, who also had friends they thought might be interested, and Memorial Day weekend was set to paint the barn and have a big barbeque. They put out the invitations and around thirty persons showed up to paint the barn. Among the working guests were Carolyn and Dick Harrison, who had moved to Topeka that spring. Dick had taken a position with the Topeka Chamber of Commerce. They arrived for the day bringing with them another able-bodied person and several six packs of beer. There are still vivid memories of watching Dick, his arm wrapped around some scaffolding at the southeast corner of the barn, with paint brush in one hand and a beer in the other, as he reached to paint the upper corner of the white trim.

The barn was completely painted by early evening and the reward came with the hanging of the huge face with the big mouth which was to become Vassar's logo, on the front of the barn with the letters over it, ***VASSAR PLAYHOUSE.***

The first season's company dubbed the face on the front of the barn "Wilhelm von Vassar." That name was given by Ric Averill, who was to meet his future wife, Jeanne Rice, when they played the boy and girl in *The Fantasticks!* the final production of that season.

Opening night was Thursday, June 18, 1970. During the last days before opening, it rained. Then, it sprinkled and rained some more. Their parking lot which had been graded still had no gravel and it was a muddy walk between the rock house and the barn. When the players arrived to begin rehearsals shortly after the first of June, they saw that much physical work needed to be done before the barn would become a real theater. When they were not rehearsing or doing technical work, sets, props, costume construction, Bruce and Dick would hand them a hammer or a paintbrush with instructions on its use. The morale was low by the last week before opening. Veda would remember a visit on Sunday, June 14th, of their friend, Don Gibson, from Winfield. Dr. Don would make many visits to Vassar during the next few years and become not only what the players would call their resident doctor, but he would also become their friend. Veda was working on the steps leading from the balcony's east door when Don asked her how it was going and she confided,

"Terrible! I don't know whether we will make it. Everyone dislikes someone and they all hate me!" And she began narrating the various differences she had witnessed or experienced over the prior two weeks. Don had sat in on that morning's rehearsal and he had seen hope,

"You've got a really good cast, Veda. The show is going to be great!" She used to trust Don's opinion. She wanted to trust it now.

"Really? You think so?" He convinced her she was unable to see the trees for the forest, or vice versa.

On Wednesday evening, during the final dress rehearsal, Veda was wallpapering one of the new restrooms with the covers of some old *Poland* magazines which she and Bruce had brought from Winfield for that purpose, when she looked out the west window and saw the sunset. She could no longer contain excitement,

"It's clearing in the west!" She called. And rehearsal stopped. Everyone came running to find a view of the west and they cheered at the beautiful sight.

The next morning, Dick was able to get gravel brought in, and a man came with a blade to spread it over the driveway and parking lot. They laid ties which had been brought in to let people know where to put their cars, and they were ready for customers!

The weather was partly cloudy; by 8:27 p.m., the sun had splayed glorious color on the clouds and the evening was pleasant and beautiful. Shortly before 8:00 p.m. Veda, who was in the dressing room getting ready for the evening, was called out to the lobby. It was Bruce telling her someone was there to see her. She opened the door, and heard singing coming from the balcony,

"Hello, Dolly! Well, Hello, Dolly! It's so nice to see you here where you belong!"

And she stepped upon stage wearing a makeup smock and her hair under a band ready to receive a wig and sang her response,

"Dolly will never go away again!"

A bus full of their friends from the Winfield Community Theater had come to surprise them on opening night.

Opening Night June 18, 1970.

The first show was *East Lynne*, a melodrama by Mrs. Henry Wood. It had at first been Bruce and Veda's idea to offer only melodramas at Vassar; but after reading many and not caring for what they read, they knew they would enjoy a variety of plays and they thought the audience would, too. As it happened, Dale Easton, who was Topeka's own *Drunkard*, had opened a theater that same spring at Lake Perry. His plate was to be just melodramas and Bruce and Veda didn't feel they had any business trying to compete with the local reigning king of that genre.

Christopher played the role of Little Willie in *East Lynne*. That show was such a long one and in those days the curtain time was a late 8:27 p.m. The cast portrayed the entire play and it lasted until nearly 11:30. It's a wonder anybody stayed to see the end! But they did. Little Willie, who dies pathetically just before the final curtain, was one night backstage with his mother getting ready for his big scene where Veda, playing the nurse, would carry the dying Willie onto stage with appropriate cries of anxiety. They were in the dressing room when Christopher's grandmother, Mimi, came in to see what was going on. She talked for a minute with Veda and then, Chris said,

"Mimi, will you hold something for me while I'm onstage?"

"Sure," and she held out her hand.

Chris then reached in the pocket of his jeans that he wore under his white nightshirt costume, pulled out a little toad and dropped it in her hand. Mimi shrieked loudly! The audience must have felt that Little Willie died early that evening.

East Lynne 1970. L-R: Roger Cummings, Janine Moody, Dick Driver, Kerry Ingersoll, Ken Harden, Marty Malik, Stacy Scott, Veda Rogers, Ric Averill, Jane Stinnett and Sandy Daily.

Veda's sister-in-law, Barbara, agreed to provide piano to highlight the action of the melodramas that season. Barbara, who plays by ear, rendered numerous tunes from her repertoire. She delighted the audiences with her command of the ivories as she appropriately announced the entrance of the villain or hero or the sweet young heroine for *East Lynne* and *The Streets of New York*. The villains were played that season by Ken Harden.

Marty Malik, a student from Ottawa University, played the roles of the hero. They were also both cast in the Moliere comedy, *A Doctor In Spite of Himself*, which came in between the two melodramas. Stacy Scott, a friend of Barbara's from New York, came to the season with some professional experience as an actress and she played the female character roles. Those three would rehearse tirelessly, trying different timing, varying the pitch of the voice or the pace of the scene, always working to see where the best result was. Before an evening's performance, Ken would walk out to the cliff just above the highway that passed west of the playhouse. He would RECITE into the setting sun and, pretending he had a cape over his arm, rehearse his leer, twirling his mustache and finally, his exit. This dedication to the art of Thespis carried over to the other players, as well, and the owners agreed they never had to wish for a better company to begin their entertaining endeavor.

Caption to right of photo: Stacy Scott *Wilkommen* pre-show olio 1970.

Life's About a Dream

The pre-show and olio were very important to each performance that first season. The evening would begin with Ric Averill taking his banjo before the audience and warming them up with a sing-a-long, or he would recite some of his stories in the voice of Donald Duck. Then, the olio would open with *Wilkommen* from *Cabaret*. Following that, the numbers would vary, depending on the show. Special costumes were created appropriately for the various numbers. Barbara Driver even got into the act with her recitation of Rose Hartwick Thorpe's *Curfew Must not Ring Tonight*. The children got into the act, as well. One number during that season was *Trouble* from *Music Man*. Ken Harden sang the lead with the rest of the company as the chorus, and one day when he noticed Christopher, who was nine, imitating him, he decided to work him into the act. He had Veda create a costume for the 9-year old to match his own and he gave Chris a cane; they rehearsed, again with the tireless energy for rehearsing that only Ken had, and that number continued to entertain the audiences throughout the run of the season.

Several of the company members discovered early on the Quenemo Pool Hall, which was located in an 1890's brick building owned by Elwood Walters, whom Bruce and Veda had known for years. After a show, the cast would say, "Well, we're off to Elwood's," and take off to play a game of pool or have a beer. One night, they came up with the idea of performing *Trouble* before the pool hall audience. Following a Saturday evening performance, everyone changed into their *Trouble* costume and piled into cars for a trip to Quenemo. Once in the pool hall, they began the piece to the astonishment of some and the apathy of others who ignored the entertainment and continued playing their game of pool or snooker. No one could say it was a success, but it was certainly an experience that provided fodder for conversation for many years to come.

Janine Moody was another Ottawa University student whose home was Topeka. She played all of the ingénue roles that season. And, Sandy Daily, from Stillwell, filled the "other woman" roles, as did Jane Stinnett, a student of Bruce and Veda's from Winfield. Kerry Ingersoll, from nearby Michigan Valley, and Roger Cummings completed the acting ensemble for that first year. Roger was also the set designer and decorator. His "masterpiece" that season came with the execution of design for *The Streets of New York*, which had one drop that looked like a snowy wooded scene, and which the owners, unbeknownst to Roger, used in several shows of future years. Roger was also a very capable actor, and his portrayal of the Mute in *The Fantasticks* was indeed memorable, especially the rain in *Soon It's Goin' to Rain*. For *Fantasticks*, Bruce brought in newcomers, Jerry Smith, Fred Eberhart and Jeanne Rice, to play the Indian, Old actor and the Girl. The show brought in crowds that were hard to top for several years after.

    Dick and Ruth and their two-year old Sara, also appeared in the olios and on stage. Everyone had to do everything. Dick even played bass in the orchestra for one show. For another, *Streets of New York*, he had the speaking role of the Captain Merriweather. Everyone's motto was "Hell, we can do that!" And they did.

Chapter Twelve

Where is the media when you want a review? The owners felt that the success of their venture lay in getting the word out about it. They also hoped the word might be positive whenever possible. They worked hard to create a good performance for every show and they tried to do an honest portrayal of the author's intent. They did not have the resources of a large stage with all the technical conveniences that a university or professional theater might possess, but they always tried to bring out the heart of the play, to present what they thought the playwright wanted. The audiences came to expect "honest" theater and when the schedule included a camp production, such as *The Boyfriend*, it appeared to go right over the heads of the patrons. The reviewers normally caught and understood any subtext which a production might have, but the reviews were not necessarily positive.

Vassar garnered reviews for most productions from the Topeka Capital Journal and the Ottawa Herald. Sometimes another paper might come in to review a show, but, although always invited, it was not something one could expect. The press usually came opening night and the reviews would appear several days, maybe as long as a week, later. Sometimes, it didn't appear until after the show had closed.

Did a good review bring an increase in the audience size? Or vice versa? Their studies didn't necessarily lead one to think it mattered. For instance, a Topeka review by Peggy Green for *The Two Orphans* in 1972, compared Veda and Bruce to the duo of Lunt and Fontanne of Kansas. (How much better can a review get?) But that show did not sell particularly well, averaging only 100, half a house. Also, it was another melodrama, which was perhaps not their bag, but who knows if that were the reason it didn't sell.

Another evening, an Ottawa reviewer for the opening of *Arsenic and Old Lace* in 1976, when the electricity suddenly failed during a propitious moment, didn't appear to realize the lights were not supposed to go out! On that particular evening a house was being moved. The electric utility, Kansas City Power & Light, had cut lines to accommodate the move, but the power company didn't warn the playhouse what was going to happen. (A complaint was made with haste to no avail!) Veda was playing Abby with Eleanor as Martha, the two aunts, for that show. They had just come to the spot where their evil nephew arrives on the scene. The lights were to dim at that point, but not go out! That performance put the stage in darkness; well, as dark as a July evening gets in Kansas at 9:00 p.m. There was, thank goodness, enough light that, where they would typically close the hayloft door above the stage so as to provide the right darkness effect, on this particular evening the hayloft door was widened to let in as much light as possible. During intermission a few minutes later, Eleanor, who always stayed at the playhouse in her trusty Winnebago, backed her camper to the barn and some new light cables were run to her generator to give light for the remainder of the show. The reviewers seemed to enjoy the special effects, and they gave the cast credit for being able to carry on!

Reviewing a show at Vassar did not seem to hold a lot of importance for many newspapers and they often did not send someone to report on the summer shows. That was, however, before Susan Menendez was appointed to review for the Topeka Capital Journal in 1976. She loved attending plays and she would make it a point to not miss any at Vassar, as well as other theaters in the area. Usually she brought along her husband, Ray and their two children, Adam and Kate. She did not always like the play or its interpretation, but she always commended the effort that went into the piece and she would find something to say that might make it worthwhile for a reader to drive thirty-five miles to Vassar to see the show. The players didn't always read her reviews of their competition, let's face it, there wasn't much time for reading the newspaper, so it is not known whether her comments on the Vassar productions were similar to her reviews of other theaters, good or bad. When she would come to review a production, whether at the barn or on the boat, she would always seek out the players before and after the show to visit with them. She became their friend, as did her husband, Ray, and the cast members looked forward to their attendance. The players always worked to give the best show in their capacity regardless of who was coming to the show, but knowing a reviewer was in the audience would help to put an edge on the production.

*   *   *

By 1972 the children, Kate, Maggie and Chris, had coined another name for Vassar Playhouse; they called it VASSAR WORKHOUSE! They always shouted it when they said it. They had been dragged from their Winfield friends for three summers and they had no social life. They were too old to be cute and too young for the older players to want them around. They were expected to hold shifts just like the grownups, but they didn't get to be in the plays, except for the few instances when a crowd was needed. Oh, they were expected to appear in the olios and they did. Chris would present his rendition of *Where is Love*, leaning forlornly against a stool that was almost taller than he, and bring tears to the eyes of his audience. And, Maggie and Kate even "surprised" a reviewer with their duet, *If Mama Was Married*. The reviewer flat stated that he had not expected to enjoy the children's act, but he did. But it wasn't the same! "You use us in the productions when it's convenient!" And they had a point.

Therefore, when Bruce was scheduled to appear on the Gerry Wallace Show, an early evening talk show on WIBW-TV, during the summer of 1972, Chris asked to go along. He said he wanted to "tell it like it is!" Bruce said, "Sure, why not?" and Chris went with Bruce into the television studio where they sat in a setting not unlike the *Tonight Show*, with Gerry sitting at a desk and Bruce and Chris in chairs next to him. After talking awhile with Bruce, the host decided to involve Chris in the interview, and he asked,

"And you, Chris? What is your job at the Playhouse?"

"Anything—whatever—" He mumbled and shrugged his shoulders.

"What about friends? I imagine you sometimes wish you could be doing what other kids your age are doing in the summertime, right?"

"I don't know what other kids my age _do_ in the summertime!" He responded abruptly and emphatically.

At home, watching the interview during their supper hour, all of the players howled at his response. They realized the advantage/disadvantage placed on the children by their parents' decision to start the theater and they sympathized. The kids were lucky and unlucky, all at the same time.

Before the first summer season of 1970 opened, Veda's good friend, Arden Andreas, had offered to keep the children for the summer so that they might continue their normal activities. Veda responded that no, she felt that the playhouse was going to be their summer home from then on and they would need to adapt as easily and quickly as possible. Arden agreed that she was probably right, but years later, Veda wondered if she and her husband might have made a mistake forcing their kids to pack each summer for VASSAR WORKHOUSE.

Guys and Dolls Finale 1972. L-R: Eric Young, Bruce Jones, Bruce Ottman, Jane Stinnett, David Rockhold, David Polson, Roger Cummings, Bruce Rogers, Veda Rogers, Carolyn Harrison, Sid Bauman, Cynthia Appley, Eleanor Richardson, Melissa Hanger, Martha Doty, Ann Richardson, Maggie Rogers and Chris Rogers.

The 1972 season opened with *Guys and Dolls*, and it involved the children all playing instruments in the mission band. Kate's real instrument was the violin and by the age of 14, she was showing a measure of proficiency, but Veda thought a wind instrument was more appropriate for the mission band, so she got out her old trombone from high school and asked Kate to try it. She showed her some positions on the slide and let her go. Her technique and tone were lacking, but she sounded okay for the mission band! Now Chris had taken up the trumpet a couple of years before and he was able to hit enough of the notes to hold his own among the ranks. Maggie, however, was already studying the flute and she took the lead with ease. As their mother would watch them from the side window while awaiting her entrance as Adelaide, she would think,

"If they honestly don't like doing this, they must be terrific actors. All three seem to take to the stage very naturally and look serious about their work." But it was time for her entrance. She took a moment to get into character and chirped, "Nathan, darling! Oh, girls, you go on ahead; I'll catch up with you later" and she wiggled her way to the stage.

The partners had invited Carolyn Harrison that season to reprise her role of Sarah Brown for *Guys and Dolls*. Carolyn and Veda had performed Adelaide and Sarah in Winfield's first season five years before. The run this summer was split with three weeks during June and then, three weekends in September. That was the first season the owners tried a split run of a show and it worked. The weather cooperated, gasoline was fairly cheap, the lake was drawing many persons that year and the show had garnered good reviews.

They were even reviewed by a Manhattan newspaper. Crowds were high, particularly the September weekends. There were chairs placed in the aisles and people sitting on the steps in the balcony, standing outside watching the show through the windows of the barn and sitting on the counter of the concession stand. The biggest crowd ever was the closing night with a recorded 240 persons in the audience.

For the June run, Carolyn was living in Topeka and would make the drive daily for the rehearsals and performance. By September, however, her husband had accepted a position with the Denver Chamber of Commerce and the family had already moved to Denver. She drove back to Kansas at the end of August bringing her little boys, Joe and Ronnie, with her, and they made their home in one of the rooms of the red trailer where Veda and Bruce lived. With school already in session in Winfield, Bruce and their three children would be making the commute each weekend. Joe was six and Ronnie, an eighteen month toddler. *Guys and Dolls* would last until September 23rd, and Joe needed to go to school. His mother enrolled him in Vassar's one-room elementary school. The bus would pick him up at the end of the driveway each morning and drop him off later in the afternoon. It was very peaceful at the playhouse at the end of a summer like that. Many of the players, who were attending schools in the area, would be gone during the week, coming in to perform their cleanup duties and perform the show on the weekends. Carolyn and Veda kept the grounds mowed and the costumes from the weekend cleaned and mended. They also tended the phone and box office. After a full summer schedule, the two friends enjoyed the quiet.

That summer had included three other shows: *Arms and the Man*, by George Bernard Shaw, the Mary Chase comedy *Harvey* and the melodrama about two young girls, one of which is blind, in Paris, *The Two Orphans*. That melodrama had been made into a popular silent film during the 1920's, *Orphans in a Storm*, starring the Gish sisters. The Vassar production had Cynthia Appley, an actress from Iowa, and Jane Stinnett as the sisters, with Jane playing the blind girl. Veda played two opposing roles, the evil old crone and a nun. Kate and Maggie were in the production as well as Bruce who played an elderly count. The other players for that season were Sidney Bauman, who played the heroic roles and Sky Masterson in *Guys and Dolls*, Roger Cummings, cast as Elwood in *Harvey*, David Rockhold, from Winfield, who acted the heavy male roles, Bruce Ottman, Bruce Jones, Martha Doty, Melissa Hanger, David Polson, Eleanor Richardson and her daughters, Ann and Beth. Three men by the name of Bruce that summer! If that wasn't confusing!

Dick and Ruth were still involved, too. Ruth had birthed a second child, Michael, in March of 1971, and the couple found that trying to care for two little children and run the summer theater, while both were maintaining full time winter jobs, became too much of a strain. They asked to be let out of the partnership in the fall of 1972, but the work and support they both provided during those first three seasons of operation can never be over valued. They continued to support the theater with their attendance over the years and, as their children grew, Sara was to spend parts of three more summers performing such roles as Baby June in *Gypsy*, 1975, Amaryllis in *The Music Man*, 1977 and Louisa in *The Sound of Music* of 1979.

Chapter Thirteen

The season of 1973 gave the entrepreneurs their first profit. The summer opened with *Hello, Dolly*, followed by *The Lion in Winter*, *The Odd Couple*, and *You're a Good Man, Charlie Brown*. Every one a winner. Almost 9,000 persons passed through the gate and, with a total of sixty-six performances, the attendance averaged 130 persons per night. The owners had calculated their break-even point at slightly under one half, or 100 persons, the theater capacity being 200 seats. When fall came, they were basking in the guise of financial success! That is not to say, however, that the summer had no problems.

The Lion in Winter. L-R: John Stricklin, Monique Debs, Joe Burgess, Mark Morehouse, Rick Rottschaefer, Sandy Eddings, and Jay Stouter.

The final show of the season *Charlie Brown* was beset with peril. The only thing that remained constant for that show was the orchestra, a three piece ensemble that sat off stage left comprised of Veda on acoustic piano, Kate on electric piano and Maggie on flute. By the end of the run, they had rehearsed the score so many times to accommodate changes in the cast, they had it memorized as well as all of the cues.

Sally Wright was in the company that season and she was understudy for the two female roles. Often, there would be no provision made in the case of a sudden change in the season. If something happened, the company would work furiously to take care of the situation as it occurred. But, for *Charlie Brown*, there had been some provisions made, because the cast knew there would be some changes at the end of the season when some players would return to school before the run was complete. The show was an extended run into the end of September. (There had been such success with *Guys and Dolls* the year before, remember?)

Bill Christie, playing Linus, commuted from Winfield and Sandy Eddings drove in from her new teaching job in Nickerson for the fall season; Joe Burgess as Schroeder, left the state to attend college; Monique Debs, Patty, was to return to her home on Staten Island; Rick Rottschaefer, playing Snoopy, had a brother getting married and he had known all summer that he would be gone for one week during the run of the show; and finally, John Stricklin, as Charlie Brown, decided to leave the show with one week to go!

Sally was able to step in and perform Lucy one or two performances when Sandy had planned to be gone, and she also completed the run vacated by Monique, in the role of Patty. The male roles were something else: Dennis McPhail, from Topeka, was brought in to do Snoopy for the week that Rick was to be gone for his brother's wedding in California, a young man from Paola, Dean Nichols, came in to fill the role of Schroeder vacated by Joe Burgess and finally, Roger Moon drove in from Buehler, where he was the drama teacher, to step into Charlie Brown's role vacated by John. Whew! Oh, and Linus! Bill Christie hurt his knee during one of the Sunday performances in September and no one, except Bill, knew it until he returned the following week wearing a <u>cast</u>! He had damaged his knee quite severely but continued on with the show! The blocking was then changed to alleviate action that would cause him excruciating pain, and somehow he stayed with the cast (and the cast)! Linus no longer glided on his knees across the floor to retrieve his beloved blanket.

Backstage there was a change, too. The show calls for split timing scene changes of many vignettes, all of which are underscored with music. Mary Stricklin, wife of John (who was playing Charlie Brown), was on tech for the show, running all of the light cues. When John left, naturally, she did, too. Twelve year-old Christopher was brought backstage to run the show and he found his niche in theater! Stage electrics!

The orchestra members were situated where there was no view of the stage; they had to "feel" what the singers were going to do. Charlie Brown's song about flying a kite is somewhat tricky, if the singer loses concentration the least little bit, he is apt to skip a large portion of the song and fly to the end. Sure enough, during one of the performances, Veda knew, even before he did it, what was going to happen—she quietly told her daughters,

"Skip to the end." They didn't know why she was giving those orders, but when they heard the singer's next line, they were ready! In fact, he didn't know he had made a mistake until they pointed it out to him after the show. It was just a "feeling," she said.

* * *

The Rogers family made application with the American Field Service to become host parents for an exchange student for the 1974-75 school term. By May of 1974, when Veda made her annual trek to Vassar early to get the playhouse ready, she knew they had been accepted to host a girl, but she did not know who the student would be, or where from. That summer marked the addition of the Whippoorwill to their summer fare and she had to oversee the acquisition of equipment, dishes and such for that operation. Mimi had offered to sew the tablecloths. Rick Rottschaefer had been hired to direct the show *HMS Pinafore* and Veda needed to get those costumes ready, as well. Rehearsals were done in Winfield prior to the season, as most of the opening cast members for the steamboat were coming from Winfield or Southwestern College.

Rick had a personal passion for the operettas of Gilbert and Sullivan and had regaled Veda and Bruce so many times singing tunes and telling the plots of many of their shows. He also felt their pieces would adapt very well to the confines of the Whippoorwill. Like those who present one-hour versions of Shakespeare, he believed he could easily strip down *Pinafore* to a delightful show not to exceed one hour. The boat was scheduled to open its season May 25th and a "test" cruise was set for Friday evening, May 24.

The summer company had all arrived that final week before sailing, and Bruce had come on Friday, following his last week of school. He arrived just in time to jump aboard before takeoff shouting, "Let's get this show underway!"

Sunset on Lake Pomona 1974.

The boat came that summer with experienced pilot and engineer. Bill Hurtig, who had built the boat, was also on board for that trial run of the season. The pilot, Glen Cunningham, rang the bells to start. Whether he gave the wrong bells or whatever the reason, the engineer threw the gears into reverse and the boat backed over the barrels which held the spars for anchoring the craft. A wharf boat would come later in the summer to serve as a dock for the Whippoorwill, but at that time she was tethered to barrels when in dock. Bruce hearing the clatter of the buckets breaking on the paddle wheel, ran back and looked over the stern. He threw up his hands saying, "What have we gotten into?"

There were still enough buckets left in the wheel that the test cruise could be made giving the cast a chance to play their show and it turned out to be a delightful evening in spite of its rough beginning. Maggie, who was then going on fifteen, played the role of Cousin Hebe. Her mother had not watched any rehearsals and, when Cousin Hebe first made her appearance on stage, Veda gasped. Martha Doty, a returning "veteran" that year heard her friend's shriek and whispered, "Your baby is grown, isn't she?" Indeed. She was wearing a dress which had been made for a previous season's female lead, and she filled it out!

During the course of that evening's run, Bruce told Veda he had received a letter from the American Field Service, telling them that beginning August 4th through the next June, they would be hosting Chantal Morin, who would become their "French daughter."

The season at the barn opened that year with *The Boyfriend*, the campy musical spoof that introduced Julie Andrews to the U.S. It was followed by William Inge's *Picnic*. And then, the season had two one-week runs, the first *A Will Rogers Souvenir*, which was compiled and performed by Avi Seaver. Next, the owners had arranged with the Walnut Valley Horsefeathers and Applesauce Association, the summer theater program at Southwestern College, to trade a show during the summer for one week, and while Vassar sent a production of Moliere's *The Imaginary Invalid* to Winfield, Horsefeathers brought *Once Upon a Mattress*, the musical by Richard Rodgers' daughter, Mary Rodgers, to Vassar.

Veda had been in the first two barn productions, playing Madame Dubonnet in *Boyfriend* and Rosemary in *Picnic*. The boat had several problems with the catering during its first few weeks; the company had begun the season making a deal with a local restaurant to fix the food which would be picked up and served by the crew. They found that there was too often insufficient food for the number of persons on board and other problems were beginning to escalate. After a few weeks Veda and Bruce felt that it would be in the best interests of everyone if they were to do the catering themselves from the playhouse. The old "Hell, we can do that!" attitude.

Veda had not been feeling very well during the first few weeks of that summer and she soon learned the reason: she was pregnant! Chris, their youngest was thirteen! She was well into the role of Rosemary in *Picnic* before they made a trip with Rick to the restaurant supply store to pick up catering equipment, all the while discussing menus for the summer and the logistics of the kitchen.

"Rick, I'm sorry but I will probably not be of much help." And she told him she was going to have a baby. She didn't want to announce it yet and she asked that he not tell anyone for a few weeks. But she wanted him to know why she was so listless of late.

She completed the run of *Picnic* sometimes running offstage to be sick in the dressing room toilet, but she got through it. Playing opposite Veda (Rosemary) as Howard was a young actor from California, Vaughn Armstrong. Jim Reynolds had returned that season and brought Vaughn with him. A strong actor, Veda felt she had to really work to keep up to his level in a scene. Several times they would come off together and Vaughn would say, "Now, that's why I came to do theater!" The scene had gone well. But she wondered if she would ever make it through the run of the play, let alone the summer yet to come!

Picnic 1974. L-R: Vaughn Armstrong, Veda, Rob Raissle, Sally Ann Wright, Jay Stoutner, Misty Maynard, Chris Edsey, and Merlene Waltner.

She had a respite during *Will Rogers Souvenir* and, with exception of helping to prepare the meals for the boat, she was able to take it easy. The following week, however, during the run of *Once Upon a Mattress*, she began hemorrhaging. She had never had any trouble while carrying the other three children, but this one was different. She would lie down a lot; she didn't feel well and she knew something was wrong. Bruce was gone to Winfield with the *Invalid* cast and she didn't know what she was going to do. One evening when he called, while telling him her fears, she began crying that something was wrong. He came home the next day. And, the next evening, after overhearing her phone conversation with Dr. Adams, Bruce rushed her to his office in Osage City. She had lost the fetus that evening. She had briefly considered abortion when she first discovered she was pregnant, and now, she was grieving that she would never know this child.

Meanwhile, the boat was doing well with catering food from the playhouse. They were performing *Tom Jones*, a raunchy little musical that played well on the boat. Jay Stoutner was cast in the title role. He had come to Vassar the year before from his home in Iowa. For the 1974 season he was also cast as Tony in *Boyfriend*, Alan in *Picnic* and Matt in *The Fantasticks*, which was the final show of the season. It had proved to draw very well during Vassar's first season four years before and the owners decided to repeat the show. Unfortunately, as was mentioned earlier, the weather was so cold during the last run of the season that year, that neither the boat nor the barn drew very well. The early part of the summer did well, however, so the end result was a little below break-even. Not too bad.

On August 8th, Veda, Bruce and the children went to Kansas City to meet their new "daughter/sister," Chantal. They had written a letter to her in June and they had received a response. She could speak English. At least, she could write English. Just to be on the safe side, Veda took along her French-English dictionary. They had received instruction to pick up their "child" at the Greyhound Bus Terminal in downtown Kansas City. My goodness, the terminal was crowded! It was the destination for AFS students for a rather large region, and there were families holding signs, "Welcome Erika!" "Thomas Family Here!" "Welcome to the USA, Jean!" "Junction City here we come!" and the Rogers family had brought no signs, just themselves. As there were several buses in the terminal, they watched young people getting off. They had received a picture of Chantal, and had sent her one of them, but would they recognize each other? Soon, they saw a slim young girl with long brown hair and glasses. She was toting a guitar and they knew! "Chantal! Here!" She looked up, smiled broadly, and a new relationship was begun.

The couple had worried about taking on a foreign student at a theater where the pace was hectic. Bruce had said, "She will either sink or swim."

It wasn't easy for Chantal. Her ability to speak the English language was not much better—oh, it was better, however—than Veda's ability to speak French. But they both would carry around their French-English or English-French dictionaries and somehow, communication was established. Chantal was shy, painfully shy. But she took an immediate liking to the Whippoorwill and was eager to help wherever needed. She became a steward on the boat. She made friends with the engineer, Bill Cason, a student from ESU (Emporia State University), and he helped her to quickly adjust to Vassar.

When the family returned to Winfield in the fall, they discovered that Chantal played the organ for the Catholic Church in her little village of Corps-Nud, in Brittany, near the west coast of France. And, Veda arranged for her to have organ lessons with Jim Strand, the organ professor at Southwestern College. Chantal was a serious student and practiced diligently. Giving her a place to practice her music was probably the nicest thing they did for her that year.

Chantal was shy—so shy, in fact, that Veda often wondered how she ever had the courage to make application for overseas study and, when accepted, had the guts to carry it through. Being thrown in with the wolves, as she was in the Rogers household, was not easy for her and there was certainly strife with her new siblings. Everyone stopped every so often, however, to take a deep breath and those respites would put the relationships back on the right course.

By the time spring rolled around and the 1975 season at the playhouse was beginning, Veda had asked Chantal where she wanted to work for the few weeks she still had left before returning to France.

"I prefer to work on the boat."

"All right. Will you agree to be in the show?"

"Oh, no, I cannot sing."

"Oh, yes you can. Everyone who works the boat this year will also be in the shows. So, which are you going to do?"

"All right, I'll be in the show." And she was, singing with the choruses for the *Riverboat Review*.

It had worked out well. In fact, upon hearing the news of the Whippoorwill tragedy during the summer of 1978, Chantal wrote her of her own grief at the news. She had returned to the U.S. the previous summer to visit her American parents (August 1977), and spent a month reacquainting herself with the family, making new friends at the playhouse and taking cruises on her beloved boat. By then she had lost her earlier shyness, or had learned to disguise it—at least, she was much more open and immediately became a favorite of the company.

For the 1974-75 school year, however, Chantal lived with the family in their late Victorian house in Winfield. The family arranged to spend Christmas in Colorado at the Gibson cabin in Green Mountain Falls. Bruce's mother, Mimi, went, too; and that trip was made with Bruce, Veda, the four children, Mimi and two dogs. Heidi and Mimi's dog, Twiggy, who was the offspring of Heidi, had to go, too! The vacation offered several unforgettable experiences. They spent Christmas Eve around a fire while it snowed outside and they put real candles on a freshly cut Christmas tree. It was the prettiest tree Veda ever remembered seeing. But, she was a sucker for candlelight!

During that vacation, the family decided to take a winter drive to Cripple Creek, continue south toward Victor and on south—on a road they had never traveled. Well, as they were driving on the snowy road, it became evident that no one else had traveled it either! They made fresh tracks. All along the 20-25 scenic miles to U.S. 50 Highway, Mimi would occasionally cry out from the back seat, "We're all going to die!" The scenery was really breathtakingly beautiful! Especially, when you couldn't see the road, the sides of which dropped very steeply. Chantal loved it, saying the mountains there reminded her of the Alps. It was an exciting journey and everyone survived.

The trip home at the end of that vacation was another experience. They left the cabin on New Year's Eve, just as Don and Judy Gibson, and their family of three children, were coming to spend the New Year holiday. The Gibson family had driven all night and snow began falling in the morning. By the time Bruce and Veda had driven down the canyon to Manitou Springs, it was almost blinding. Bruce continued the drive and when they left Pueblo east toward Kansas, it was already mid-afternoon. Cars and trucks were stranded on the highway and in the ditches. Finally, the family made it to Syracuse, Kansas, where they rented a motel for the night. It had taken them a whole day to drive half the distance to Winfield, double the time it would normally take. The next morning, they got up early to continue their journey home only to learn that the snow had ceased at Syracuse!

For the season of 1975 the couple decided to offer an opera, and *The Medium* by Gian Carlo Menotti was selected. It is a short tragedy, approximately 40 minutes long. They selected *The Bald Soprano*, Ionesco's classic in theater of the absurd, to balance the evening. Veda had directed *Medium* at Southwestern a year before, with Jennifer Warner in the lead as Baba and they asked her to repeat the role. Kathryn, who was sixteen, sang the role of the young girl, Monica. She was young, but she handled the role well, and Veda was very pleased with her daughter's rendition.

Playing the piano for the piece was Veda's niece, Deetra Driver, who had joined the company that season. She had also played for the opening musical, *A Funny Thing Happened on the Way to the Forum*. Both have quite demanding scores and Dee showed she could handle them. During the run of *Medium*, she suffered a burn on one of her hands while working her cook shift. She played the show—a painful performance in the most literal sense.

The last show of that season was *Gypsy* and by the time the rehearsals began, it was hot and very dry. At that time, one of the chores of the day was to collect trash and burn it in a barrel fashioned into an incinerator. Although the players had been cautioned not to burn during windy periods, someone did. The wind carried some burning debris into the prairie behind the rock house and it caught fire. There was a nice cabin about seventy-five yards north of the playhouse and, the fire swept into a roaring blaze within a few minutes of igniting. As the wind was blowing the blaze north, the rural fire department was summoned and everyone stopped their business to get old blankets, tarps, buckets, whatever, to fight the fire. Greg Clevenger, who was pilot of the Whippoorwill that season, said he had fought mountain fires in his home state of Arizona and he knew what danger they held. It was a frightful day, but, with the help of the fire department, the blaze was stopped.

Or was it? During supper that evening, someone called, "Fire!" And everyone rushed outside to help. Evidently, there was some underbrush that held some live embers and they re-ignited with another blaze. The players soon had it out and began their evening preparations with some taking turns to check on the prairie every so often. On the boat that evening, Veda, who was in the show, told their audience of the day's fire fighting activities. Following the shows that evening, Bruce had scheduled a rehearsal for *Gypsy*, since they had not been able to run it earlier in the day due to the fire. Around 1:00 a.m. came the dreaded shout, "Fire!" And everyone had to stop for the third time to fight yet another fire. This time the fire department was called for the second time. The blaze, although not as high as the first one had been, was beyond their tired energies. The firemen stayed to ensure they had gotten all of the embers and everyone went to bed!

One of the shows on the boat was a review called, *A Night in Algiers*, which Chris was in. One evening, during Will Hladik's rousing rendition of *Ahab, the Arab*, Chris took over the boiler watch while Larry Springer, the engineer, was to make an appearance in the show. The fire for the boiler was always something fearful; it seemed to burn in spurts, dying down appearing to go out, when there would be a *boom* and the flame would flare up—or out, sometimes. The engineer who tended the boiler always had to watch the gauge and the height of the fire and the steam pressure for the generator, making adjustments wherever needed to try to keep every thing on an even keel. Chris was tending the boiler when the flame flared *OUT*. He was wearing a skimpy pair of pants and the flame caught both of his legs. Realizing what had happened, he flipped off the fuel switch, ran up the steps to the landing and jumped immediately into the lake. That action probably saved him from some severe scarring. He had first and second degree burns on his legs and had to stay in bed for a week, not to mention the fact that his legs were very tender the rest of the summer.

Chris was scarred one earlier time, during the summer of 1971, when he was stung by a honeybee. Evidently, he had never before been stung. At least, his mother never remembered such a reaction as he had that summer. His face swelled to the point of deformity. Bruce rushed him to the doctor within minutes of the sting, but he remained swollen for several days. Although customers had thought they knew the children, when they would see Chris that week, they would ask, "What's wrong with that little boy?" not even realizing who he was.

It was during the summer of 1975 that a "tap-tap-tapping" sound would be heard coming from the stage late at night. Jan Feager would relax in her tap shoes. Will Hladik and Lynn Gordon met that summer and would become another Vassar romance. Rick Brown and Linda Conway, who had come from the Mid-Continental Theater Touring Company, stayed on that season to produce *The Apple Tree* for touring to area schools in the fall. The idea came about too late in the season to get enough schools and had to be scrapped later on. Paula Harryman, Barbara Driver's niece, came from Denver to do the costumes and play the role of Connie in the Neil Simon comedy *Come Blow Your Horn* and Mazeppa in *Gypsy*. Jan Feager was Louise in that show with Lynn Gordon as June. Also in the company were Larry Goodwin from Winfield, Monty Mesecher, Dennis Anderson, a teacher from Lyndon, Paul Bannan, David Dietz, Brian Evans, who played the blind Don in *Butterflies are Free* and Toby in *Medium*, Nancy Moulds from Hutchinson, Eleanor and Ann Richardson, Dennis Rafferty, Karen Somers and Keith Pickering who played Lycus in *Funny Thing* and Mr. Martin in *Bald Soprano*.

Chapter Fourteen

Cooking the dinners for the boat as well as the company meals became part of the daily routine starting in 1974 with the purchase of the Whippoorwill. A cook would be hired each summer to plan the daily meals, assist with ordering food and cooking the company's lunchtime meal. The cook would also ensure that food was on hand for breakfast and supper, but the player on KP for that day would have to see to those meals plus the clean up from all of the meals for the day. The cooks became favorites of the players. First, in 1971, there was Eunice, who drove out from Lyndon each day. A soft-spoken woman, the players soon realized she was able to read palms, and they would ask her to read their palms. They could always tell if she saw something that gave her worry, and they would kid her about it, trying to get her to tell them, "What do you see, Eunice?" But she would never let them know her fears. She always managed to switch the topic or wiggle out by saying, "You realize, I am not a professional at this, and I don't always know how to interpret the lines I see." Okay.

Eunice was the company cook for four summers, and then came Ione McFadden, also from Lyndon. Ione often brought along special treats when she came for the day. Those treats might include some fresh vegetables from her garden, or some cookies that she just happened to make the night before—always, something. Another special lady, Ione was the company cook just the one year, 1975.

Next was Janelle Warren, the sister of Nelson Warren and Carolyn Harrison. That was 1976. Their parents were then living in Admire, so Vassar was convenient. Janelle had spent a year in Japan and brought some of their cooking techniques to the playhouse.

The next two summers, 1977 and 1978, brought Jennifer Warner, Vassar's own Julia Child. A talented singer, Jennifer had spent part of 1975 at Vassar, singing the role of Baba in *The Medium* and again, in

1976, she spent a few weeks while singing in the chorus of *Oklahoma*. She had, by then come to establish a bond with many of the players and she made her job fun. Once during the summer of 1977, she and Diana Gish woke the company late at night with their *disco cooks* routine. They dressed in sunglasses and headgear, calling themselves "Eunice and Ione," and beat wildly on pots and pans, waking everyone. Having never known Eunice and Ione, they didn't realize the desecration they had created in their characters, but the performance did give everyone a good laugh and something more to talk about that summer. Jennifer brought her own cooking techniques to the summer company. She couldn't simply cut up a chicken, she would hold it aloft and begin beating it with, "I'm going to attack this chicken!" Always good for the morale.

The Company 1977. Back L-R: Nelson Warren, Tom Mitchell, Kay Reeder, Larry Pressgrove, Marcheta Willhite, Jeanne Fridell, Bruce, Paul Bannan, Roger Aday, Jennifer Warner, Diana Gish, Kevin Fewell, Jim Olson, Chris Rogers, and Max Fridell. Front L-R: Judi Sterling, Julie Krieckhaus, Dido (German Shepherd) Eleanor Richardson, Joi Hoffsommer, and Kate Rogers.

During the summer of 1978, Jennifer was the company cook, and she also played the role of Golda in *Fiddler on the Roof*. With the help of Veda, she planned the meals for the boat and scheduled the cook shifts, deciding what needed to be done when and how many persons each shift would take. During the cook shifts for *Dames at Sea*, Maggie was assigned to do the French bread. Jennifer taught her how to make bread, "It's good for aggression!" and she would punch and beat the dough. Each day they would assign a name for the bread—on June 17th, Maggie named it *Gone with the Wind*.

Chapter Fifteen

"All right, everyone on stage! We are going to take the company photo!" Bruce called the company together. It was the last night of the season and the group would likely never ever be all together again. At well past midnight, they had finally completed strike of both the boat and barn shows. *South Pacific* had ended the season at the barn, and a barbershop quartet from Ottawa, *The Sound Alternative*, had played the final week on the Whippoorwill. The group, made up of a music teacher, printer, lawyer and a financial advisor, had continued to entertain throughout the hours of striking the barn show, even after performing a full show on the boat. It was just after they had regaled Veda with her favorite, *Shenandoah*, that Bruce convened everyone for the photo. The troupe began arriving, one by one, onstage, weary from the evening's work. They had taken apart the sets, swept the barn and stage, sorted and cleaned costumes, put away properties, stored dishes and kitchen utensils for the winter. They had even "wintered" the Whippoorwill and secured it to the wharf boat.

They grouped together, forming different levels—some sitting or lying on the floor down front and the next row standing, the next, on a platform and, finally, Veda and Debbie Kramer topped stepladders. Veda was usually the company photographer, but in 1978 one of the players, Brad Johnson, served that role.

The summer held so many memories—all different for each player. Their faces showed the strain of the strenuous prior months, as well as the joy in the friendships made that summer.

Greg Thomas, who had come to the summer from Laramie, Wyoming, sprawled on the floor in front of the seated first row of players. Diana Gish leaned in, with her right elbow on Greg, against Chris. Next to him was his sister, Kate, who had already returned to Southwestern for her second year and who would turn twenty the next month. Next to her was seated

Susan Sublett, a Baker student, and Maggie, who would return to ESU for her sophomore year. Then came Julie Krieckhaus, holding a bottle of wine left over from the season, and Larry Springer and Jennifer Warner.

The second row situated themselves, Alan Daymude, another Southwestern student, Deborah Bremer, who was attending Ottawa University, David Ollington, from Manhattan, Grant Fuller, a graduate of OU, and Kay Reeder, Southwestern, who had come in to play piano for *South Pacific*. Behind that row were Julie Hall (Veda had lots of memories of singing with her father in a college dance band back in the '50's) from KU, Larry Pressgrove, Patty Wirtz, who had played Nellie Forbush in *South Pacific*, Aaron Gragg, Roger Aday, another KU student from Wellington, and the quartet from Ottawa, Bob Green, Darrel McCune, Mike Esser and Paul Dexter.

Squeezing in behind them were Jim Olson and Eleanor Richardson. Further back were: Bruce, standing on a chair, Tom Mitchell, Linda Waltz, Mark Swezey, Debbie Kramer, Bernie Wonsetler, Steve Strohm, a high school student from Lyndon, Veda, and finally, Doug Duncan, from Lecompton. Doug's parents were perennial season ticket holders and he had been seeing shows at the country playhouse since he was a little boy.

After the photo, each collected the address of the other saying, "Now don't forget to write." Some cried and some laughed. They all had other lives and would be leaving the summer behind.

The company slept in the next morning, Labor Day, and took their time cleaning quarters and moving out. Eleanor drove Kate and Chris back to Winfield. Chris had made the decision to live with the family's former neighbors, the Martins, to finish his senior year at Winfield. Veda and Bruce drove Maggie back to Emporia and by evening only Jennifer Warner was behind. She wanted to finish the cleaning and storing of the kitchen by herself. She would depart the next morning, leaving Vassar Playhouse to Bruce and Veda.

The couple spent the next week giving their yellow trailer a facial uplift. They installed new carpeting and re-organized the kitchen to hold just enough utensils for their personal use, not for catering meals for 50 people!

On Friday, September 8th, their 22nd anniversary, Bruce and Veda drove to Winfield.

"Come on, Hunk!" Kate shouted. She was sitting with her parents as they watched the Winfield vs. Newton high school football game and

Chris was on the field. He had earned that nickname during the summer. He had appeared in *Come Back, Little Sheba* in a cameo role, and the players began calling him, "Hunk." The coach soon replaced him with another player, but Winfield won the game!

Bruce and Veda and Kate spent the weekend at their home. They had sold the house during August to a Winfield pharmacist and his family. The new owners would take possession the first of October, and Veda had arranged for movers to come in the end of September. Kate spent the weekend helping her parents pack up the home.

"I have a role in the fall musical," she told them, "I'm to play Esther, Noah's wife, in *Two by Two*."

That was a show that the couple had never done and did not know. The theater department at Southwestern College had changed, with a new director hired for the fall of '78. Kate was eager to start rehearsals. Since graduating from high school, she had felt it was a waste of time for her to go to school, as all she ever wanted to do was to be on stage. It was an argument she and her mother often had.

"Kathryn, I want you to be prepared to support yourself *offstage*. You are musically talented and have the skills for the violin. You can always get a job in the pit, if you are not hired for a role." The argument was an old one that both had memorized.

They had other conversations that weekend while packing away their personal things. "Kate, must we take these rocks in your closet?" Bruce's voice bellowed from his daughter's bedroom.

At some point in her childhood she had begun collecting rocks. Her parents never knew when or why it all began, but anytime they would drive to a *new* place, she would bring home a rock. Bruce had the year before joked that her closet would one day fall into the dining room, it was getting so full of rocks! Well, it hadn't fallen and the thought of packing them and paying for the movers to transport them to Vassar did not please him.

"Well, if you can take a box full of bricks for your books, you can take my rocks!" She had a point, and so he agreed to move the collection to Vassar where it would be stored with the family belongings in a refrigerator car until Bruce and Veda had their depot built for a home.

"It seems so strange not to think of ever living here again." Katie, along with her brother and sister, loved the family home. They had lived there for over twelve years and Veda remembered their reactions upon seeing it for the first time.

"Sweetheart, this marks the end of your childhood," her mother responded.

Their neighbor, Miss Karr, who had served as the children's third grandmother, had died in July. Bruce and the girls had been able to visit with her in the nursing home where she lived her last two years when they had brought *Dames at Sea* to Winfield. She died a few days later. The whole family drove back to Winfield in two vehicles to attend the funeral. Kathryn sang for it and she, Chris and Maggie needed to get back to the Playhouse for the evening show, while the parents drove to Nickerson for the burial. Between the Whippoorwill and Tina's and Miss Karr's deaths, Kathryn had been given life's crushing blows that summer, and she was like Peter Pan. "I don't want to grow up. I don't want to see you get old or Mimi and Grandma Driver die." Veda remembered the words of nine-year old Kathryn from years before.

"Think of this change as a new opportunity," she told her daughter. They finished the packing and Bruce and Veda went back to Vassar. They told Kate and Chris that they would be back in two weeks to finish the moving.

They returned to Vassar to begin the renovation of the railroad cars. One by one they had been moved to the corner during the summer. The three passenger cars had all suffered fires at some time in their service and their condition caused many curious questions from the customers. Bruce and Veda would respond with a request that they wait until the next spring to pass judgment, as the couple planned to spend the winter repairing and decorating them.

They hired a local electrician to help plan the heating and cooling. A restaurant equipment firm came out from Kansas City to plan the kitchen, and they had already contracted for that to be done. The SBA, in fact, had cut checks for work as soon as it was ordered. Everything was beginning on schedule, insofar as they had planned, at least.

The weekend of October 8th, the family came together for a dinner at Ruth and Dick's in Topeka. Veda's family had developed a tradition of celebrating different occasions together, but in October, they always had a dinner to celebrate their mother's birthday, October 6th. They also said the dinner was for <u>all</u> the October birthdays, and that included Kate, October 2nd, and Mimi on October 11th. (Although Bruce's parents were not technically part of Veda's family, they had often participated in the Driver family dinners, sometimes when neither Veda nor Bruce were present.)

The family gathered on Sunday, and Dick and Ruth's house in Topeka was filled with relatives. Veda's nephew John Friesen was there from Houston, Texas. He offered to drive the children back to Emporia and Winfield, as he would be going that direction on Sunday evening, and Veda accepted the generous offer. The family car, a 1973 Chevrolet station wagon, had been acting up since the end of the summer and they realized they were going to have to trade it in soon! It was not dependable.

"I think I will go out to see the train. I have not really even seen it yet!" Kathryn exclaimed.

"What do you mean you haven't even seen it? It has been sitting here all summer!" her sister responded.

"Well, I know it, but I never took the opportunity to go out to look at it."

The children went out to the train following their return from the family dinner, to take advantage of the daylight and see the train before it got dark.

Bruce walked through the cars with them and explained his vision of how it would look. "This is *Ocean View*, the kitchen car. We're going to put a big door here that will lead to the deck that Jim Gardiner built last summer. The deck will be the place where food deliveries are made and there will be a large pantry and walk-in cooler."

Once the tour was complete, they returned to the yellow trailer to get ready for the trip to Emporia and Winfield. John arrived as scheduled and the parents made their goodbyes, promising to see the children in two weeks when they would go to see Southwestern's production of *Two by Two*, with Kate as Esther.

* * *

"I have to get my driver's license renewed and I'm scared," Mimi said to her son when she was visiting the following week. Her birthday was October 11th, and this was the year to renew her license. Bruce deliberated. On the one hand, it might be just the right time to have her stop driving; but on the other, it was nice to have her somewhat independent. They had begun to realize several years before that she was sometimes forgetful and incoherent, but she managed to keep going and getting around. She was, however, another reason they had decided to make the permanent move to Vassar. Veda had acknowledged two years before that her mother-in-law couldn't manage her checkbook and she had taken over that task, helping her to pay bills and reconciling the bank statement.

"Maybe if Mimi doesn't pass her driving test, I could have her car?" Kate had asked her parents. The idea was tempting to Veda. It would be nice to have a car in Winfield for Chris and Kate. On the other hand, they didn't need the added expense or worry that another car would cause.

"Okay, I will help you to study, Mimi," Bruce answered. And, he began drilling her on the items listed in the drivers test manual.

Bruce drove her to the sheriff's office the next week to take her test. When he came back to the Playhouse, he sought his wife, saying, "She passed." It was with both relief and dread in his voice.

In the meantime, Bruce and Veda were shopping for a new car and they finally decided upon a small 4-cylinder 1978 Mazda 2-door GL. It was a far cry different from their huge gas guzzling Chevy station wagon, but they were ready for a change!

On the 21st of October, they picked up Mimi, in Quenemo, and Maggie, in Emporia, and the four drove to Winfield to see *Two by Two*. As their old home had by now sold, the couple and Mimi stayed with their friends, Wayne and Jane Cherveny. Maggie stayed with her sister at the dormitory, and Chris was with his second parents, Vic and June Martin. They all went to see the show at Richardson auditorium. The couple was impressed with their daughter's performance and they told her so. The role of Esther is more adult than any she had previously portrayed. In fact, Esther dies in the process of the play, and that scene was particularly believable and moving.

The next day Kate told her mother that she was planning to enter the National Association of Teachers of Singing (NATS) competition in Pueblo the first of November, and she wanted her mother to go along and play for her.

"What are you singing, Kate?"

"I'm not sure yet, but I'm working on *O Mio Babbino Caro* and *Après Un Rêve*."

Veda was familiar with both songs. She had heard the Puccini aria many times and the latter, by Fauré, she had taught, at least once, to a student. "I don't know, Kate. We are already behind with the train. I am not sure I should leave again," she answered.

"But I want you to. Please, Mutti?" She would often call her mother by the German familiar appellation for mother when she really wanted something.

"All right, if you are that set on my going, I will come back on Wednesday, November 1st, and we will drive to Colorado on Thursday." And she got her way.

The couple then departed for home with Mimi and Maggie.

Chapter Sixteen

"I am special. I *am* special." She was very quiet. They had been driving for over seven hours and were in Colorado nearing Pueblo for the weekend of the NATS convention. There was a long pause.

"Are you all right, Kate? How do you feel?" her mother asked.

"I feel like I've been in a cage all these years, and someone just opened the door," she answered, "I'm free!"

"We've never known when we should tell you. I've never wanted you to feel handicapped in any way; and, in regard to your being molested, Dr. Scott said at the time that I should let you forget it. Now I don't think that was a good idea. Throughout your life since the age of five, your father and I have listened to you cry out at night in fear of something you could not describe. I believe now we should have told you much sooner."

She had been telling Kate the story of her childhood: the illness she had suffered when she was almost three, and the neighbor who molested her when she was nearly five.

The illness had been something the doctors could never explain. One Friday morning in early August 1961 Kate awakened with her eyes out of focus. They were suddenly crossed for an unknown reason. Her parents also noticed she wasn't running. They called the doctor that morning and he stopped at the house on his way to the hospital. He examined her and watched her for awhile before saying,

"She seems pretty normal, except for her eyes being crossed. I think you'd better get her to the eye doctor."

"But, Dr. Scott, she isn't running. She just walks." He explained that, because she wasn't able to see clearly, she may be more cautious. Half-heartedly accepting that explanation, she made an appointment to see an eye doctor for that afternoon.

By the time Kate had awakened from her nap, she was having a hard time walking. Veda took her to the appointment with the optometrist, who examined her and said,

"There is something wrong in her brain. I can't help her."

Early the next morning, her parents heard, "I fall down and can't get up."

Veda arose and went to the girls' room to find Kathryn in a heap by her bed. "Katie, what is wrong?"

"I can't get up."

Veda lifted her daughter into her lap and sat on the bed which was wet.

"Kathryn, you don't wet your bed anymore!" She was surprised.

"I'm sorry."

That afternoon the girls were playing in the yard by Bruce as he washed the family car, when Kathryn fell down again and was unable to get up. Bruce picked her up and took her into the house. He started to cry as he said, "Veda, we must get some help. This isn't normal."

Again she telephoned the doctor and he asked her to "wait and see."

The next morning they went to church, as usual. Kathryn had to be carried everywhere as she couldn't walk at all. By noon, both parents agreed they could wait no longer for medical attention. Veda telephoned the doctor at his home and explained the problem.

"All right," he sighed, "Bring her to the office. I'll meet you in 10 minutes."

The doctor was probably normally a very patient man, but Veda reasoned she had tried his patience earlier that year during Christopher's birth when she had false labor pains and went to the hospital *three* times before he was finally born. On the second trip, when the pains stopped, the doctor had decided to induce labor. He had sat with her while the pains were going really good and when they stopped, he told her to go on home.

"You're not going to have that baby this weekend. I've seen many mares before they drop a foal. You don't have that lean, drawn look yet."

"Dr. Scott, I am not a horse!"

"Well, in any case you are not going to have that baby this weekend. I'm going to go on to Kansas City to the NCAA tournament." With that he left her room.

Veda ended up walking the six blocks from the Junction City Hospital to her home on South Adams, lugging her suitcase and crying the whole distance.

On the third trip in the early hours of Sunday, March 19, 1961, the doctor was out of town, and Chris was delivered by the doctor on call. When he returned from his trip on Sunday evening, Dr. Scott saw Veda walking down the hospital corridor to view her son through the nursery window and said,

"Are you still here?"

"Yeah, but I had results this time!" And she pointed to her baby in the nursery.

So, on that August Sunday morning Veda felt she had given him reason to sigh and she tried not to let the impatience in his voice upset her as she put Kate in the car and drove to the doctor's office. Once there, she walked around to the passenger side of the car to open the door. She started to pick Kate up when the doctor said,

"Let her down to walk."

"But Dr. Scott, she can't!" She then stood her daughter on the grass where she crumpled into a small heap.

"Oh, my God! What's wrong?" He rushed to pick the child up and they entered his office where he began his examination. Her reflexes were not normal. She had no feeling in her legs and very little in her abdomen.

"That explains the wet bed this morning," her mother stated.

When he asked her to hold something, she grasped it, not with her fingers, but with the palms of her hands. The doctor asked, "Does she usually hold objects this way?"

"Of course not, she is able to use her fingers."

The examination lasted just a short while before he was on the telephone calling the University of Kansas Medical Center in Kansas City, to have her admitted. Kate had a paralysis that was obviously progressing. He wanted to be sure she would be in capable hands if the paralysis went to her lungs. When he was off the phone, he asked if the couple would have trouble finding places for the other children to stay. He offered to keep them.

"No, I have family in Topeka. Someone will surely be able to keep them."

Veda returned home and the couple hurriedly packed enough clothing for a few days for themselves, as well as the children, and they left for Topeka where Christopher, who was six months old, was deposited with her sister, Peggy, and 20-month old Margaret with her brother, Don. Because they felt time was of the essence, they gave very little explanation, as they, themselves, didn't know what was happening. They just knew they had to hurry and get their oldest child to the hospital. They then continued on to Kansas City.

It was very frightening for the little girl, as well as for her parents. She was in the hospital for ten days with every specialist in the area probing on her at some time or other. And, they ran tests and more tests. Her condition was a puzzle. After a few days, the doctors decided she was not getting any worse, and Bruce made the decision to round up the other two children in Topeka and return to Junction City. In Topeka, after picking up Maggie, Peggy talked him into letting her keep Chris a few more days. He gratefully accepted the offer. After more testing and probing, Kate was dismissed and she and her mother returned home.

She still could not walk and she had lost control of her bodily functions, but slowly Kate began to improve. She would soon crawl up and down stairs and, before many weeks passed, she began walking again. Dr. Scott later confessed to Veda that, on that Sunday when she had brought Kate to him, he didn't know whether she would come home in a box or not. And he also told her, "Sometimes on my way to or from the hospital, when she is playing in the yard, I just stop to watch her for awhile." He called her his miracle patient.

And she did improve. Slow progress. Years later, the family had moved to a new home, and she was in the fourth grade before her teachers stopped asking her parents at their first parent-teacher conference if there were something wrong with Kate's coordination. And Veda would begin the saga of her mysterious illness. It took three days for her to get it and almost seven years for it to go away. In the spring following Kate's hospital stay, when on a routine visit to his office, Dr. Scott informed her that he had finally heard from the KU Medical Center.

"What was the diagnosis?" she asked.

"They termed it post infectious encephalitis, which is a condition arising from a childhood illness such as chicken pox or measles."

"But, Dr. Scott, she didn't have any measles or chicken pox last summer."

"You know that and I know that. Their diagnosis is wrong. I think it is more likely she somehow contracted an unidentified virus. We may never know what she had."

Then something else happened. Two years later, during the summer before Kathryn started kindergarten, she began having horrible nightmares.

She would scream and fling herself around. When her father approached her at these moments, she was uncontrollable. She would squeeze her little body into very tight places screaming about the *green giant*. Her parents couldn't figure it out. Otherwise, during her waking hours she seemed a very happy and outgoing child.

Toward the end of July that summer, one morning when she was cleaning the sleeping porch, Veda heard her daughter screech, "He wants me to touch his penis!"

She looked out to see an old man dressed in overalls in her neighbor's yard. The neighborhood children were gathered around him. Calmly she called her daughters, "Kathryn! Margaret! Time to come inside."

As soon as the man left the yard, she asked the older neighborhood children about him and learned that he was a friend of her elderly widower neighbor in the back. While she was talking to the children, however, one of the older girls began to tell her of another retired neighbor who had taken an interest in Kate and was taking her into his recreational vehicle for her to play from time to time.

When they were alone, Veda questioned her daughter carefully. The answers she provided, coupled with the frequent raging nightmares exhibited by the child, gave Veda all the proof she needed to realize that her daughter was being repeatedly molested by the neighbor. After a brief conversation with Bruce, they telephoned the police.

Mr. Belgrade, the neighbor, was at that time a recently retired army major whose job was to administer various tests, such as polygraph and psychological testing. At the time of the complaint, he was out of town with his RV, but upon his return, the police called him in. He denied the charges and they asked him to take a lie detector test. He did so and passed. Based upon that one test, the police called the parents back into the station. The police had concluded the innocence of Mr. Belgrade and asked the parents to apologize to their neighbor!

The couple had, in the meantime, also told their back yard neighbor of his elderly friend's actions with the neighborhood children. When confronted, the man confessed saying how lonely he was. He displayed senility and confusion. Upon learning of the incident, his family obtained help for their father. Veda could only feel compassion for that old man.

Prior to the incident in the back yard, however, Veda had taken Kate to the doctor for her pre-kindergarten examination and vaccinations. Dr. Scott noticed that her pelvic area was red and swollen. Veda asked him what might cause that and also told him that Kathryn had sometimes complained of a burning sensation around her vulva. (Little Kate knew the terminology.) He suggested that she might be "playing with herself."

Later, however, Veda talked to the doctor again, reminding him of that earlier visit, and asked him if he felt she could have been molested. He responded that there was probably not penetration, but yes, fondling could certainly have caused the irritation. She told him of meeting with the police and their reaction to the incident. She asked what she should do.

"You could press charges and take him to court, but Kathryn will have to testify. The court must wait until she is five before she can testify (six weeks) and putting her on the stand could be more trauma than she has already suffered. I suggest you let her forget it."

* * *

So, she had never told her daughter until now, fifteen years after the fact, as they were nearing Pueblo, Colorado.

"I know now that you have never really forgotten. Maybe it is impossible. After you grew up, I often wanted to tell you, but never did really find what I felt was the right time. Tonight I felt it was right."

"I'm just glad you've told me now."

"Anyway, Kate, that is why your father and I have always felt you were rather special."

"I am special. I am special. Please, God, please—don't let me be *normal*." And they both laughed as Veda found the Ramada Inn, where they checked in for the weekend in Pueblo.

The next morning, Friday, the 3rd of November, at breakfast they ran into Larry Pressgrove, who was also attending the auditions. The convention was held at the University in Pueblo. Everything was new and the buildings looked like they arose right out of the desert. After attending some of the sessions and after hearing Larry's audition, Veda took her daughter shopping. She bought a pair of boots. Jennifer Warner was also attending the auditions and they went to hear her sing.

On Saturday morning, Kate got up very early to be ready for her audition at 9:30 a.m. The judges chose the Fauré *Après un Rêve* for her to sing. Veda opened the short piano introduction and Kate's voice began the plaintive French song. Full of sadness and longing, the poet tells of his desire for the night wherein he is able to see his dead lover in his dreams.

As she listened to her daughter sing, she couldn't help the pride she felt with her child's performance. After all, it had been less than two weeks since she had sung the role of Esther in *Two by Two*. The letdown following a theater performance is very natural and she knew that Kate was tired and suffering from post-performance syndrome, but it certainly didn't show in her singing. It was clear and lyrical, a beautiful performance.

Afterward, several acquaintances who had been listening came up to offer their congratulations to Kate on her singing. They all wished her well with the results. At noon Veda fully anticipated finding her daughter's name on the list for the semi-finals, but it was not there.

"I'm just as glad," Kate said, "I think I would rather be able to enjoy the other performances and not have to worry about my own." But Veda was clearly disappointed, for, having been a teacher of singing for many years, she felt her daughter's performance had merited the semi-finals. Larry's name was not on the list, either, which was also puzzling, but Jennifer's was, so the two attended her audition where she sang wonderfully. They also attended the finals for Kate's division just to hear the competition. Again, Veda couldn't understand how Kate was overlooked. She felt her daughter's singing certainly matched, if not surpassed, many of the contestants in the finals for her division.

Kathryn wasn't disappointed. She said she'd had a headache all day anyway and was glad she didn't have to perform more than the one time. They went back to the hotel where Veda read the critique sheets. The rules are that, with three judges, a contestant has to receive two scores of at least 90 to qualify for the semi-finals. Veda read the scores. There were two scores in the 90's. Kate *did* qualify, but somehow her scores were overlooked and her name omitted from the list. That restored confidence and made her mother even more proud!

On Sunday, they made the long drive back to Winfield. After dropping Kate off at the dormitory, Veda picked up Christopher to take him out for a sandwich before she continued to Vassar. Veda told Chris how the train was coming along. Bruce had painted the exterior of two of the cars, and, although the interiors were still burned out, at least they looked good from the highway!

When she arrived back home later that evening, Veda found Bruce had also painted the caboose which shone a bright red in the evening glow as she pulled into the lane. She related her weekend to Bruce and told about seeing everyone. She said she was glad Kate had insisted on her going.

The next afternoon, Kathryn telephoned that she still had her headache and that she had awakened that morning seeing double and had numbness in her fingers and toes.

Her mother caught her breath. "No, Kate, that is impossible. You are imagining that. You must be. Have you seen a doctor?"

"Yes, I saw the school nurse who sent me to the Snyder Clinic. Three doctors looked at me and told me to go home and sleep it off." Kathryn responded, sounding very scared.

"Sleep what off?"

"I don't know. I think they thought I was on drugs."

"Katie, go to Dr. Kaufman, if you feel you need to see a doctor. At least he knows you and has some history to go by. I'll call you tomorrow to see how you are." She told her goodbye and hung up the phone. She boarded the train where Bruce was working on wiring for the kitchen and she told him of the conversation.

"What is she going to do?"

"Well, she will see Dr. Kaufman tomorrow if she isn't any better. We'll call her again tomorrow."

Veda did call at noon on Tuesday, but she didn't talk to Kathryn. She talked with a friend who asked her to call Dr. Kaufman. The doctor said he had examined Kate and felt she might be suffering from a migraine syndrome. He was a migraine sufferer himself and shared some of the symptoms she had displayed such as nausea, numbness, blurred vision, etc. He said he had prescribed medication and had requested a brain scan for 9:00 a.m. the next day.

Chris telephoned that evening obviously shaken. He had seen Kate after school and was terribly worried about her. Veda called Kate immediately after their conversation. Again, she got the friend she had spoken to that morning. She asked to please talk to Kate. There was a long wait before an unknown voice slurred,

"Hullo?" Very slow speech. She talked with her daughter, asking questions, and Kate said she thought the medicine made her groggy and that she would be all right the next day. Veda agreed, but asked her to call or have someone call after the brain scan in the morning.

The next day, Wednesday, just before noon, Dr. Kaufman telephoned to tell what he did not know. Kate was beginning to have trouble swallowing and he couldn't explain it. He had admitted her to the hospital that morning. Veda asked if she and Bruce should drive down.

"I am unable to find anything wrong, but if it were my child, I think I would."

Bruce and Veda were in Winfield three hours later where they found their daughter on an I.V. She couldn't talk, but she could communicate by nodding her head "yes" or "no." She also let her parents know with gestures that she was numb. She said she was unable to drink or swallow.

The parents visited with the doctor who said all of her tests were normal and there was no sign of infection. He wanted to run more tests in the morning and a brain scan. Veda said that she needed to talk to him about the illness Kate had when she was almost three.

"It had a lot of these same symptoms and worked very rapidly. She was confined at the KU Medical Center for ten days in isolation, while they ran tests and really found nothing wrong. But it took her seven years to get over it." The doctor was interested in the history and said he would request the report from KU.

"But, the odd thing is we had never told her of that illness until this past weekend when she and I went to Colorado. Could she be imagining this illness?"

"Oh, no, I don't think so. I think this is real. It certainly appears that way."

On Thursday, the parents found their daughter no better. The doctor had ordered a nasal gastric tube to be inserted to remove mucous from her lungs and enable her to breathe more easily. They sat with her and Veda accompanied her to her brain scan, which was completed about 1:00 pm, at which time Eleanor then came to the hospital. "I thought I would sit with her for awhile, if you had something you needed to do."

Bruce and she went to lunch and both got haircuts. Veda returned to the hospital at 3:30 pm and relieved Eleanor.

Shortly thereafter, Jim Strand, Kate's theory teacher at Southwestern, stopped in to see how she was doing. And, David Herrin, who had played the role of Noah in *Two by Two*, also stopped as he was visiting his grandfather across the hall from Kate. She was in good spirits, but Veda sensed she was very tired, so when the visitors left, she closed the door to Kate's room. She talked with Kate for a few minutes and swabbed out her mouth. The nurse came in and took her temperature.

"You're very tired, aren't you, Sweetie?" And Kate nodded.

"Why don't you try to get some sleep?" It was shortly after 4:00 pm, and Veda sat in a chair beside her daughter's bed and watched her. Bruce and Christopher came at 4:30.

"She seems to be resting now. I need to go to Southwestern to talk to some of her friends. Maybe she has been on drugs."

"That is always a possibility, but they have been testing her for substances and haven't found anything," her husband responded.

"Well, I want to talk to them anyway. Maybe I will learn something." She took Chris and they left for the dorm. They had just walked into Sutton Hall, when someone called to Veda,

"You need to get back to the hospital. Your husband called for you."

She and Chris jumped back into the car and rushed back to the hospital.

"What it is?" she asked, when she reached the floor of Kate's room and found Bruce in the hall.

"I think she has died," he whispered. "Right after you left I found she wasn't breathing and called the nurse. The doctor is putting her on a respirator."

They cried and hugged each other. "No, no!" After a few moments, the doctor appeared.

"We have put her on a respirator and all of her bodily functions appear to be working normally. I have made arrangements to transfer her to the Wesley Medical Center in Wichita, where she will be seen by a friend of mine who is a vascular surgeon. There may be a blockage that I am not seeing"

Mike Marion, who had married a Vassar player from 1976, Cindy Wesley, and who was now the campus minister, drove the couple to Wichita, following closely behind the ambulance. As soon as they reached the emergency entrance and Kathryn had been transported to the Intensive Care Unit, Veda sought one of the emergency medical technicians who had accompanied their daughter in the ambulance.

"Tell me, how is she?"

"All vital signs are good," he responded.

"How long can a person be without oxygen and still survive?"

She wanted to know how long had she sat in the room watching her daughter, thinking, no, totally knowing, that she watched her chest move up and down as she breathed. Had she died the moment Veda had encouraged her to go to sleep? Would they be able to revive her? Would she be all right, if they succeeded? She had so many questions and no answers.

Eleanor came to the hospital in Wichita wanting to help.

"Tonight is the opening night of *Guys and Dolls* at Emporia. Maggie is one of the Hot Box girls. We were all supposed to see it on Saturday.

Would you mind driving to Emporia to pick her up after tonight's performance and bring her down to the hospital? She will want to see Kate." And Eleanor and Larry P, who was attending Wichita University, drove to Emporia.

Another play opening that same night was *Born Yesterday* at the Winfield Community Theatre, and Wayne Cherveny was one of the leads. Bruce and Veda had initially planned to come to Winfield on Friday, see that play, then, with Chris and Kate, they were to go to Emporia on Saturday to see Maggie's show.

The night in ICU was a long one. The couple took turns going into their daughter's room, talking to her and hoping she could hear and respond, visiting with the nurse and watching the machine that displayed all of the vital signs. And they sat in the waiting room and visited with those who came by. Chris came in with his best friend, Victor Martin, who was attending the university in Wichita. Chris had somehow gotten to Wichita, too, Veda didn't remember. The parents told them that Maggie would be coming in around 1:30 or so. Chris said he would come back to see her.

They held hands and remembered. Veda would say later that it was the most intimate night she ever spent with her husband. They talked and shared thoughts of their firstborn all night long.

"Maybe we are lucky to have had her these seventeen years," Bruce stated, out of the blue, and Veda asked, "What do you mean?"

"I mean that she could have died when she was almost three—or, she might have perished last summer with the Whippoorwill. Maybe we are lucky that we've had her this long."

"Why is it that life has to be such a drama for us, Bruce?" She asked.

"What is that supposed to mean?"

"Well, we can't do things simply—our fathers died within two days of each other—and then, last summer I thought the Whippoorwill was enough drama for the rest of our lives—but, no, now there is Kate!"

They continued sharing their feelings, laughing and crying together.

Eleanor, Larry Pressgrove and Maggie came in around 1:30. They hugged each other and then took Maggie in to see her sister. She had been in a coma since 4:30 that afternoon.

"Talk to her, Maggie. The nurse says the patient sometimes can hear and understand. If it's possible, Kate does, I know." And she left Margaret to be alone with her best friend.

Chapter Seventeen

From Veda's diary, November 10, 1978.

Kate died this morning at 10:30 a.m.—rather, the respirator was removed. She actually died yesterday afternoon at 4:30 p.m.

We went back to Wayne and Jane's in Winfield to make arrangements. Carlyle Spohr and John Blythe for the service, The Southwestern College A Cappella Choir—Don Gibson—Ross Williams—etc. etc. Katie. Katie.—

Many callers tonight We sent Margaret back to Emporia for Guys & Dolls.

The hospital will do a post mortem. We gave up Kate's eyes and kidneys. Somehow she will live on.

Joe and Barbara have brought Mimi to Winfield.

* * *

Two of the callers on Friday night were Lee and Joan Kaufman. Lee (Dr. Kaufman) pulled the parents aside, "I know you've requested an autopsy. Perhaps we will learn something. But I think that the disease she contracted was going to run its course, regardless of what we could do, to her death. We couldn't stop it."

Veda pondered on the thought of pre-destination. Maybe Kate had always known she was not going to be here a long time. She recalled a trip a couple of years earlier when she was driving her daughter to KU after a semester break and Kate was trying to convince her mother to let her quit school and go to New York. They had been discussing the Playhouse and Kate had complained that she never got to play leading roles at Vassar. "But what about the roles of Nick in *A Thousand Clowns*," Her mother asked, *"Or, Monica in The Medium?"*

"I was convenient for you in both cases," she responded.

"Convenient or not, you received good reviews for both shows which you deserved. Don't be in such a hurry. I didn't play a lead role until *Pajama Game*, when we were in Junction City, and I was 27 years old," her mother continued.

Then, Kate burst, "But, don't you see, Mama, I won't be here!"

Veda very nearly stopped abruptly on the turnpike. "Whatever do you mean?"

And Kathryn began citing passages of scripture from Revelation about the coming of the end of the world. Veda tried to allay her daughter's fears by saying that fanatics had preached the end of the world for centuries. "Of course," she said, "The world does end every day for someone." But she believed Kate had every reason to expect many years ahead for herself.

As she remembered that conversation, she began to feel that Kate sensed intuitively all along that her life would be short. And, maybe, telling her about her childhood was to fill in the puzzling gaps about herself. Maybe that information did indeed free her daughter. Death is a normal fact of life, but it can be very harsh, especially, when it takes a child before her parents.

On Saturday, Margaret helped her parents clean Kate's dorm room. They packed the clothing in boxes and found her music and violins in her locker at the Fine Arts building. Several students stopped by to offer condolences to the grieving family.

Eleanor, Larry and Tom Mitchell spent the day calling players, and Eleanor arranged for all of them to sleep at her house. Veda and Bruce had made funeral arrangements the day before, and it was scheduled for Monday. Veda's brother and sister-in-law, Jim and Betty, would be bringing Hannah, her mother, down on Sunday. So many friends had opened their houses to the family, and Jane scheduled those arrangements.

In the evening, Bruce, Veda and Mimi took Margaret to ESU and to see the production of *Guys and Dolls*. The conductor, Howard Halgedahl, had been head of the orchestra and string program at Winfield when Bruce was first hired in 1966, and he was a good friend of the couple. As they watched the performance, Veda could not help marveling that she was able to enjoy the show. But, she thought, that is what Kathryn would want.

After the show was over, the couple approached Howard, who beamed when he saw his old friends, "Well, how are you? Maggie didn't say you were coming tonight! And how is Kathryn?" Kate had been in his orchestra as a junior high student.

They relayed the news and he was overwhelmed that Margaret had said nothing. "And you both came to the show tonight?"

"Well, Maggie knows the show must go on. She didn't tell anyone, because she wanted to be able to maintain her composure through the performances." We told him how her friends had been picking her up each evening to convey her to Winfield—and then, back for the next evening's show. It was as if she had two different lives. That is how the theater works, and she found it therapeutic to wrap herself up in another character for a few hours each day.

On Sunday, more people from out of town arrived: John, Carole, Steve and Scott Lynes from Minneapolis, John and Carole had been Kate's Godparents, Jim and Betty, Dick and Ruth, and Veda's mother. She hugged her mother and said,

"I think I now have some feeling for what you've gone through all these years." Veda's brother, Bill, was killed during WWII and Veda had many memories of her mother, years afterward, crying when she would read a story or poem about a young soldier. She felt her mother should "get over it." She had eight living children! Veda was to learn that one *never* gets over it, but that doesn't prevent a person from enjoying life without the loved one. We all possess a drive for living, with the good, bad and all the changes.

Margaret was staying the weekend with the players at Eleanor's. At first, her mother felt hurt that she didn't want to stay with her parents at the Cherveny's. But then, she realized that Maggie needed the players' support, and it was healing for her to be with them. Besides, Wayne and Jane had a houseful, with their own children home for the funeral, as well as Bruce and Veda. Their friends had given over their own bedroom and king-sized bed. And they took such complete care of the couple—food, laundry, whatever was needed. In fact, Jane, who owned the best dress shop in town (and she was having to work as usual every day), asked Veda if she had brought a coat, because the November weather could turn cold for the funeral. No, she hadn't brought one, it was warm when they came down. So, Jane brought a coat home from the store, and Veda purchased a new coat. Jane even tended to the dressing of Kate's body and styling her hair. Veda could never have imagined such friendship.

It is strange how things seem to work out. The Southwestern A Cappella choir had held a concert performing Randall Thompson's *The Peaceable Kingdom* the previous weekend, when Kate and Veda were in

Colorado. She had known she would not be in Winfield for the concert, so she hadn't rehearsed the piece. For the funeral, the choir sang selections from that work, and it was appropriately perfect. Many of Kate's friends from the Campus Players served as pallbearers. As she sat with Bruce in the pew of the First Presbyterian Church where their children had grown up, Veda had to smile at the drama of the ordeal—her numbness—the gut-wrenching grief—the hurt. The unmitigated truth—Life really is a melodrama.

The church had acquired a new minister during the previous summer and, because they were not yet acquainted with Carlyle Spohr, they had asked John Blythe, the minister at the Baptist Church across the street, to assist with the services. Their children had gone through school together. Bruce had chauffeured their son, David, along with Maggie and other students, to early morning rehearsals many times. Also, Veda and Donna Beth Blythe had sung together in choirs and quartets and attended music club together throughout their 12-year Winfield tour. They felt so comfortable with the Blythes and were certain John would know the right words to say over their daughter.

After the services at the church, a dinner was served for the family who then made their way on the journey back to Quenemo where Kate's burial would be in the Driver family plot at Oak Hill Cemetery.

The couple and their two remaining children drove the three-hour trip. Mimi had wanted to travel in the same car as her son, but the Mazda was too small for five persons. Also, Veda wanted the privacy, if possible, of only her immediate family, for that last journey for Kate.

The weather was nice. It turned cooler as they drove north, but the sun shone and it was still a beautiful day. The family shared their memories as they made the familiar drive through the Kansas Flint Hills. They even attempted for a short while to play the familiar game of *name that tune*. The children had grown up in a house where music played constantly, and they had become very familiar with many shows. Their game was for the one who was "it" to sing a brief phrase and the others would need to name the show, the character who sings the tune and the composer. It was a game at which Kathryn had become particularly proficient. At one point in the game, Veda exclaimed that she suddenly had the distinct feeling of Kate looking over her shoulder.

At the graveside services more players appeared. John Blythe officiated the service in the cemetery. He and his family had lived just a few blocks west of the Rogers home and their children had done so many things together—it felt right that John should be the one to conduct her body for burial.

The Quenemo Ladies Aid held a light supper for everyone following that service. And, afterwards, their friends began to disperse. John and Steve Lynes drove to Kansas City to catch a flight back to Minneapolis, but Carole and Scott stayed, as did Eleanor and Maggie, with Veda and Bruce in the yellow trailer. They spent the next morning writing thank you notes, and Eleanor returned Maggie to Emporia for school. In addition to being in *Guys and Dolls,* she had been cast as Louisa in *The Fantasticks* which would open in a few weeks, and she had rehearsals starting that week. Carole and Scott left the next morning very early and then, just as Eleanor was leaving in the afternoon, Carolyn Harrison arrived with her mother.

Carolyn had flown from Denver for Kate's funeral, but the route was varied taking her to Tulsa and on into Arkansas. Somehow she finally made it to her parents' who were by then living in southern Kansas, in Galena, but she was too late for the funeral. So, her mother drove her to Vassar, where they spent a couple of days with the bereaved parents.

Meanwhile, the Rose Restaurant Supply from Kansas City had suddenly appeared to begin work on the kitchen car, and life would go on, numb or not!

One week later, as the couple was working, a car from the sheriff's department drove into the lane. Veda walked out to meet the trooper.

"What can I do for you?" She recognized the deputy.

"Hello, Ma'am. I have to serve you these papers." And he was gone as quickly as he had appeared, leaving her with a large envelope.

She stood in the parking lot and watched him drive off, as she opened the letter. It was a notice of lawsuit pertaining to the Whippoorwill. "Bruce!" She cried, as she entered the train car where he was working. "I cannot believe this. Now we're being sued!"

He stopped what he was doing and they walked back to the yellow trailer where they sat and read the papers. "What should we do?" She asked.

"Let's call Stu." Their attorney, Stuart Entz, had cautioned them in the fall that lawsuits were a probability, but they had not believed him. How could anyone sue them over a natural disaster? Bruce telephoned the lawyer who said, "Yes, I thought this would happen. You just send me a copy of what you have received. You will no doubt receive more summons.

It will be hard, I know, but do not even think about the papers. Just send a copy on to my office and you two take care of your healing. You've had enough. You don't need to worry about this, too."

Thanksgiving was spent with Veda's family at her nephew, Roger and his wife, Ann's new house, which they had completed the prior summer. Veda's Aunt Wilma, was visiting from Colorado, and her mother's two other sisters, Florence and Lucy, who were both in senior care centers in Topeka, were also at the family dinner.

Veda found socializing to be extremely difficult. She wanted to be left alone. She wanted only to read and sleep. A high school friend of the couple, Colleen Engle North, who had grown up just a half mile east of the Playhouse, came to visit them. She had been living in Philadelphia the year before when her young son was killed in a freak auto accident while serving in the military in Australia. Following the news of his tragic death, the family had to wait nearly two weeks before the body could be brought home for the funeral and burial of their only son and brother. Veda had sung for that funeral and she recalled her drive back to Winfield following that service, how she wept that her friend had to suffer such a loss. Colleen brought many books with her when she came to visit, and Veda read them all and still had questions that couldn't be answered.

On the Friday after Thanksgiving, many players arrived. Jim Olson had organized a work party and they came to help build the train! Bruce was ready to begin installation of the outside windows in the parlor car, so he accepted their offer and gave them each a job. The weather had turned beastly cold during the week and there was no heat in the train cars. Well, in the car where they were working, there weren't even any windows! They shivered and shook—and when it became too cold for them, they joined Veda in the yellow trailer, where she was cooking lunch, to warm up. Then, they would go back out and try again! The help was great. Before the day was done most of the windows had been installed. Bruce invited them all back over Christmas vacation to join him for a glass of wine in the parlor car and they agreed!

The couple tried to continue business as usual, but their grief slowed them down. Like the last song she had heard her daughter sing, Veda longed for dreams that might bring her daughter to her. She slept a lot; at least, she stayed in bed. And she read and read: books of near death experiences—books on healing and the after life—books on grieving parents. Slowly and painfully she was able to face each new day.

Meanwhile, Bruce was having trouble on the train. The workers from the Rose Restaurant Supply seemed so cavalier about their work. Sometimes they showed up, most times not. It was the end of November and his patience was wearing thin. Bruce confronted Veda,

"Let's go to KC to the Rose Restaurant Supply and meet with the owner. This has gone on far too long!" They made the trip to Kansas City and to the restaurant supply firm.

"I want to talk to the owner."

"He isn't here."

"I insist on talking to someone with authority!"

"The president is in."

"He will do!"

After a period of waiting, a young man appeared and took the couple to a place where they could talk.

"We signed a contract with your company last summer to complete a kitchen installation. We have a check ready to give you upon completion, and your people keep giving me the run around. This one is sick. Another is on vacation or no longer works for you. The job was to take six weeks and it is now over *three months*! I don't know what the matter is with you people, but I am ready to take our business elsewhere." Bruce expressed his displeasure.

"You say you have a check?"

"Yes, I do—the SBA has already written the check for your contract." And Bruce produced the piece of paper with full payment.

That got the young man's attention. He promised that the couple would have workers on site the next day and they would get the job finished in a timely manner.

The workers did show, and the kitchen car had its equipment in time to cook their Christmas dinner, but it was not without struggle and problems. One day Veda was entering the train when she overheard her husband shouting at the workers,

"What is it with you people? Is this job so difficult? You were supposed to finish it last October! It has been over three months! I am fed up! I've endured a tornado that overturned my boat, I am being sued and I feel like my guts are being torn out over the death of my daughter!" And as tears welled in his eyes, he ran out of the train, nearly knocking over his wife.

Always amazed at his ability to communicate his feelings so strongly when pressed, Veda felt profound compassion for her husband. She had been selfish in her own grief and he needed help, too. So many of the books she was reading dealt, not only with the death of a child, but also, the separation between parents that grief causes and the divorce that so often follows. Were they going to become another statistic? How could they avoid it? As young parents they had joked, "If you divorce me, you have to take the kids!"

Then they purchased Vassar Playhouse and, it was "—take the playhouse." Then, "—take the boat." Maybe that joke was healthy for them. Now they could say, "—take the train!" They needed to get through this winter and somehow survive together.

By Christmas they had received several summons of lawsuit, they didn't try to keep track of how many they received, and more continued to arrive throughout the winter. With each new summons, they would simply mail a copy to the attorney and go on with their lives. They invited Mimi and Grandmother Driver to join them for Christmas dinner on the train. The electrician had installed one of the heat pumps, the one for the parlor car, and Bruce had installed a wood burning Franklin stove. It was for atmosphere, as well as warmth. The name on the parlor car was *Cendrillon*, French for Cinderella. It had probably originally been a smoking car, or club car. In any event, the name implied *sit by the fire*, and the couple had decided to do just that with the installation of the Franklin stove. Bruce and Veda cooked their turkey in the new restaurant range in the kitchen car and Chris and Maggie served the plates to the waiting grandmothers in the parlor car, which was the only car with any heat at the time. The cars still had no decoration, but infrastructure was nearly done—the plumbing and wiring.

On the weekend after Christmas, as they had promised, many of the players arrived and were served some leftovers and wine in the parlor car where they held their own Christmas (or New Year's) party. They were eager to talk about the next year's season. In spite of their grief and the work on the train renovation, Bruce and Veda had somehow managed to get the 1979 schedule set and a mailing out for the annual season ticket drive. They had invited Tom Mitchell to be managing director and he had accepted. They talked with him about the season which would open with *Kiss Me, Kate*, the Cole Porter musical he had pressed the owners to do for years. They discussed inviting Carolyn Harrison to perform the role of Kate, and Bruce and Veda wanted Tom to do the Petruccio role.

* * *

John and Carole Lynes invited the family to spend New Year's with them at their cabin on Mount Princeton in Colorado. They had often seen the New Year in with their long-time friends. Once, during a visit to their Wichita home after Christmas 1975, John had asked,

"What are you doing for New Years? Why don't we drive out to the cabin together?"

And they did. Steve had undergone knee surgery a few weeks prior to that evening, and he was in a right leg cast that extended from waist to toe. Bruce and Veda said they could drive their station wagon. They thought everyone could get in if they strapped the luggage to the rack on top. So, the four adults and five children made the journey to enjoy a brief holiday in the mountains near Buena Vista, Colorado. Steve had to ride in the middle seat with his leg stretched across whoever sat to his right. The station wagon had three seats, so they could position three in front, four in the next and two would ride in the rear seat which faced not where you were going, but where you'd been. It was a great time and both couples had fond memories of those days when all were together.

Now, in 1978, John's work had taken their family to Minneapolis. His mother and Carole's parents were still living in Wichita, so they made periodic trips that direction. Bruce, Veda, Maggie and Chris agreed to meet them at John's mother's house in Wichita. And for this trip they drove two cars to the cabin on Mt. Princeton. Veda took her camera along and took photos of everyone. One has Steve sprawled in the snow wearing his cross-country skis, no cast for this trip. The photo looks like he is deceptively upright, skiing downhill.

Although very grateful for her friends' solace and generosity in sharing their retreat, Veda continued to mourn her daughter's passing. It was not something she could set aside and be able to go on with her life. Her eyes continued to express the dull ache of the bereaved. It was something she would later come to recognize in the eyes of other grieving persons.

After the holiday, she and Bruce made the drive back to Kansas with their two children. They left Christopher in Winfield with Vic and June Martin, and together with Maggie, they returned to the playhouse. Maggie still had a few weeks of vacation before school would resume. Before the Christmas holiday, they had been able to catch her performance of Louisa in *The Fantasticks!* It was wonderful. Her voice lilted on the top notes just as easily as on the ones in the middle voice. And her *I am special* speech was just as Kathryn would want. Kate had wanted to play the role of Louisa since she had first seen the show at Vassar in 1970. When the players again performed it in 1974 with taped accompaniment, Kathryn had run the sound equipment for that production and, by the time it ended she had memorized the show. She would be very pleased and proud of her younger sister's work.

As they neared Vassar, they encountered a lot of snow. The highway had not yet been cleared, but there were many tracks and the Mazda had no problem. The lane to the Playhouse, however, was something else. The snow was over a foot deep in places and Bruce didn't know whether to try the slope of the lane or not. "Nothing ventured, nothing gained," he said as he threw the car into second gear and roared up the lane. They made it.

When she unlocked the trailer and turned on the light, she gasped at the sight before her. Veda always had lots of green plants around, sitting on the counter, hanging in the windows, etc. Her plants were all frozen! And it was cold in the yellow trailer.

"What happened? Why is there no heat?" He exclaimed. And he went back to the furnace and found it off. At the bathroom door, Maggie exclaimed,

"Look at this!!" Her parents joined her to find the stool had run over and frozen. It looked like Mount Vesuvius caught by surprise! What had happened?

Everyone has a choice when dealing with difficult situations. Certainly the couple had their fill of tribulation at this point. But, this present situation, in comparison to what they were dealing with emotionally, was not serious. The three of them stared for a while at the ice in the bathroom and then, they all began laughing. The trailer looked absolutely ludicrous with its counter full of dead plants and an ice sculpture in the bathroom. And it was freezing cold!

"I can't deal with this now. We are going to Mimi's for the night." Bruce was on the phone calling his mother to leave the door unlocked for them.

During their vacation in Colorado, the power company and the electrician had changed their service to 3-phase. Bruce confronted the electrician the next day who confirmed that the switch was indeed made.

"Oh, I checked your trailer before I left. Everything looked fine to me." Bob, the electrician, stated.

"What was the temperature that day?" Bruce asked.

"Oh, it was unusually warm, in the 70's I guess." Uh-huh.

Evidently, the furnace had gone out with the switchover, but because it was so warm, he didn't notice that it was out. What's another problem, more or less?

Bruce lit the furnace, turned off the water to the trailer and Maggie got out the hair dryer to thaw the bathroom. Once it was cleaned up, dried out and the plants tossed, Veda brought in the beloved *Sylvia* for their necessary relief. Bruce would not be able to run new water lines until spring; but they didn't care. Veda said she could melt snow or draw water from the well and they would just have to take sponge baths for a while. Borrowing a large pot from the Vassar kitchen, she kept a pan of hot water on the stove the remainder of that winter. The couple would become somewhat fond of their two-seater outdoor privy.

After returning Maggie to ESU, the couple was invited by Sally and Rick to see them in a play that Dale Easton was presenting in Topeka. While they were at Vassar the previous summer, Rick had obtained a teaching job at an elementary school and the couple had moved to an apartment in Topeka. Following their performance, the couples were visiting over a cup of coffee.

"We are going to get a divorce." It was an abrupt announcement by Sally. She went on to explain that they had tried, but their marriage was not working and they had mutually agreed to give it up. Rick would move out and let Sally keep the apartment. He asked to bring his cat, Big Kitty, and move in with Veda and Bruce. The stunned couple pondered for a few moments before Veda said,

"Well, there is the old *Warm Morning* wood burning heating stove that I grew up with in the garage at Joe and Barbara's. We can put it in the bunkhouse. Then, we can turn the water on there. You could stay there, Rick, if you will allow us to use your bathroom and take a shower occasionally." They relayed their recent woes and it was agreed.

Rick and Big Kitty arrived the next week. He joined the couple in their work to restore the train. One of the projects was the windows of the parlor car. The car would have double windows. The outer ones were installed by the work group of players at Thanksgiving, and Bruce had created a design for the inside panes that he would have sand blasted, resulting in etched windows. Their evenings for the next few months were spent around the kitchen table in the yellow trailer, cutting out the designs with X-Acto knives. The process was to first cover the panes with two layers of a clear plastic film, being sure to smooth out any air bubbles.

Then, Bruce would lay on the stencil he had created and spray paint it over the plastic. Finally, Veda and Rick would painstakingly cut away the parts that were to be sand blasted. They hoped the process would work, but it would be several months before they would know for sure.

Veda found the hours she spent with Rick to be very therapeutic. They shared a lot of memories. He told her of his own tormented childhood, his mother's suicide and his long estrangement with his father, who was a successful surgeon in Palm Springs, California. He marveled at all of the visible memories Veda had of her children.

"I have only one childhood photo of myself." And he produced a small photo of himself at two or three years of age seated in a high chair.

"Oh, we are very fortunate in that area. We have many photos of all stages of Kate's life. We even have her voice and violin on tape." And she put one of the tapes on the player to share with Rick.

Rick also helped Bruce on the train. He wanted to be of use. He offered to stay on during the summer to set up and run the bar. The couple accepted his offer. They spent the winter with choosing the decor for the train, such as the fabric for the Pullman dining car. It was the green car, a sleeper with the name of *Clemenceau*, and the oldest of the three passenger cars. They learned that it had been put into service shortly after World War I, as a French statesman of the time was Georges Clemenceau.

Veda was at that time also on the board of directors for the Association of Kansas Theater, otherwise known as AKT. The annual conference and auditions were held in Wichita and Bruce and Veda made the trip to attend. While there, they shopped and found carpet for the train and ordered two patterns, one for the dining car and the other for the parlor car.

There were also trips to Topeka and Kansas City to choose wall coverings and light fixtures for the cars. They had decided to decorate the caboose, which would house the bar, in the covers of old sheet music. The couple had boxes of sheet music, much of which had interesting covers. They hired two young high school students, Steve Strohm who was in *Fiddler* the summer before, and Keith Robinson, to work after school and on weekends to perform various jobs. One of their assignments was to paint trim work and grain it to look like mahogany. They used that process for the interior of the dining car, even graining the steel berths which now housed the ductwork for heating and the lines for plumbing and sound. The interior of that car was all painted a rich deep mahogany.

They purchased quarry tile to put in the kitchen and they began the process of wall papering the parlor car.

The cars all sported hogback roofs and the interior ceilings curved on the sides to meet the walls. The curved area in the parlor car had been covered with a layer of tin to take out the unevenness where walls that once stood had been cut away (long before the couple had purchased the car). Bruce and Rick set about wallpapering those strips, approximately 30 feet long. They laughed as they struggled with the long strips of striped paper, making sure they were going straight. When done, they both admired their work before turning in for the night.

The next morning early, Rick walked over to the parlor car to admire their prior evening's work before setting out for his teaching job in Topeka, and he came running back to the trailer with a shout, "Come quickly, the wallpaper all fell down!"

Sure enough their hard work was lying on the floor of the parlor car. Bruce wondered what could be wrong and he telephoned the local lumberyard for suggestions.

"Did you prime the metal?"

"No, was I supposed to?"

"Oh yes, wallpaper won't stick to bare metal. Paint it first with a thick coat of paint, latex will work." They had so much to learn.

So, that day he set about priming the curved ceiling, and the next evening he and Rick tried again. Veda straightened out the pre-hung strips and pasted them again. This time, the paper stuck and they could continue with the walls.

Meanwhile, the couple made periodic trips to Winfield to see their son compete in wrestling. Following Kathryn's death, using proceeds from life insurance, they had sent a contribution to Southwestern College for use by the A Cappella Choir. A touching note of thanks from the director, their friend Warren Wooldridge, had explained that the money would be used as a scholarship. They received an invitation from him to attend a special memorial service for their daughter in March, with the choir's performance of the Fauré *Requiem*, one of Bruce's favorite choral works. They attended the concert with their children. It was a moving service with beautiful music by the choir. On the turnpike, as they made their way back home, they felt very touched that the school would so honor the memory of their beloved daughter.

"How many people do you know that are honored by a live performance of the Fauré *Requiem*?" She asked her husband.

"Only President Kennedy that I can think of right off, his memorial was with a performance of the Brahms *Requiem*" he responded.

"Well, she's right up there with the President." she quipped.

Chapter Eighteen

They had set Easter weekend of 1979 for the opening of the Vassar Shortline. Good Friday, April 13th. In March they hired a chef from Topeka. He would arrange the kitchen, pantry and walk-in cooler, and help to set the menus and order supplies. He was also going to train the stewards. Veda purchased fabric and sewed long dresses covered by simple long white aprons for the women staff, and she purchased jackets for the men. They were trained in how to greet their customers, how to make them comfortable, how to carry the food, how to present it and when to clear the table. The owners wanted the performance on the train to be every bit as pleasing as the one in the barn, and they worked hard to get a good performance from the staff.

On Thursday, April 12th, they hosted a trial run, a VIP dinner, inviting those firms and persons who had helped them to create the train. The chef was in the kitchen car busily preparing his *specialite'* for the evening. And Veda and Bruce were in the dining car, laying the Alexander Smith carpet they had so carefully chosen the prior month. Not to miss a deadline, they finished covering the floor a little less than two hours before the evening was to begin!

The guests arrived, were greeted by the entrepreneurs and seated at the new tables on the green upholstered seats of the *Clemenceau* Pullman dining car. And with appropriate "oohs" and "ahs," there were many questions. Most of the guests were able to answer the questions, as they all had something to do with the project and were able to respond to the area of their own expertise.

The guests seemed to enjoy the evening, the dinner, and the atmosphere, and the evening was a success. Following the departure of their VIPs, the owners and staff sat down to relax and recap the evening. Just like the rehearsal of a play, Bruce gave his notes.

"Stewards, you must be careful when someone is in the aisle. Don't try to pass the customers. You must be aware of each other, however, and allow each to pass. Hot food has priority."

He had other instructions, many of which would not have been noted without the special rehearsal dinner. They parted knowing that their work lay ahead for the real test, with real customers!

Vic and June Martin arrived the next evening for the grand opening of the Vassar Shortline, bringing Christopher with them. The doors of the restaurant had opened for lunch at noon with fourteen customers. Not enough to be profitable, but they felt it would grow. For the first evening, however, they had eighty-five diners and it seemed to be off to a promising start.

By the time the summer season at the barn opened, they felt like restaurant pros. The evening meals were coordinated with the shows at the barn, somewhat like they did on the boat. For instance, during the run of that season's *The Sound of Music*, the coordinating dinner was Wienerschnitzel. Veda blew up photographs from each show to be glued to the back of the evening menu.

Many players returned from the previous season. Carolyn Harrison came in to perform the title role in *Kiss Me, Kate*, and there were also Deborah Bremer, Joi Hoffsommer, Tom Mitchell (the Managing Director for the summer), Debbie Kramer, Jim Olson, Larry Pressgrove, Mark Swezey, Eleanor Richardson, Nelson Warren, Margaret and Chris. Newcomers for the season included Barbara Meier, Kelly North, Kim O'Brien, Beth Velasquez and Jan Zabel. Rick Rottschaefer and Karen Swoyer and Chef Henry Wahwassuck handled the train staff.

It was during the run of *Cactus Flower* that Bruce and Veda realized their chef had problems bigger than they could handle. He was drinking on the job, there were reports of him receiving kickbacks from suppliers, other reports which Bruce and Veda could no longer ignore. On Sunday, July 1st, they met with the man early in the morning. Before they could say anything, he announced his resignation, and Veda gave him his final wages.

Since the beginning of the summer, Bruce had been somewhat in charge of the Sunday brunch, and it was normal for him to be in the kitchen early Sunday mornings, baking the rolls and making the cream puffs for the weekly brunch that was becoming more and more popular with the customers. He decided to take over the kitchen fulltime and fill the role of chef for the Shortline.

The company again tried to hire a piano player for the season; and once again, it didn't work out. So Veda supplied accompaniment for *Kiss Me, Kate*. Jim Olson directed *The Sound of Music* and had cast her in the role of the Mother Superior; the piano duties were shared for that show. Jim also felt it would be good to have an accordion for certain segments of the production. So, Veda asked around and found an accordion which she borrowed from an old high school friend and neighbor to the Playhouse. With the "Hell-I-can-do-that" attitude, she quickly learned how to play the accordion—simple tunes, that is. The accompaniment was split between her, Larry Pressgrove, who was also playing the role of Rolf, and Bruce, who could vacate the kitchen and come to the theater at the end of the show to play the finale, when the whole cast was on stage. Bruce also made an appearance on stage as an extra toward the end of the show, but he felt he could be out of the kitchen by that time and be able to play the finale.

One evening, dressed in her nun's habit, while awaiting the start of the show and her first entrance, Veda sat on a chair on the concrete pad behind the shop by the train. She had her wimple off and her voluminous skirts were pulled up thigh high as she attempted to stay as cool as possible before sweating it out on stage. Oblivious to the world, she regained consciousness when she heard a woman's laugh,

"Are you in the show, too? Or, have you recently taken your vows?" It was Susan Menendez who was just coming off the train to review the evening's performance. Normally, no one entered or exited by that door on the train and Veda hadn't expected to see anyone other than cast members. Susan had visited with her a little earlier on the train as she greeted the customers and helped with the serving of the evening dinner.

"Oh, yes," Veda answered, "I'm holier than thou in this show!" And they both laughed, all the while Veda hoping that the reviewer would not say anything of her unprofessional behavior!

The summers are hot at Vassar, there is just no getting around that fact. On several occasions during particularly hot spells, various players had succumbed. One was Lynn Gordon who passed out while working in the sun one day during the season of 1976. Someone found her and revived the young actress bringing her to a shady place where they plied her with fluids. The heat is not good for any age, and caution was always given to the players at the beginning of each new season.

Veda had another experience during the run of *The Sound of Music*. One evening, while singing *Climb Every Mountain*, she noticed Maria's eyes twinkling with laughter, and the audience also was sniggering. What was wrong? Was her wimple crooked? Not being Catholic herself, she was totally unfamiliar with how a nun's habit should be worn. Had she done something wrong? Oh, it was humiliating to have to keep on singing that great song of inspiration and not know the cause of laughter all around her. With the scene's end, she tromped into the dressing room. On her heels came Deborah Bremer, who was playing the role of Maria.

"Do you know that you had a spider on the top of your wimple?" Deborah laughed.

"A spider?"

"Yes, while you were singing, a granddaddy longlegs was crawling slowly around the top of your wimple. That's what everyone was laughing about." Puzzle solved.

The last two shows of the 1979 season were *The Diary of Anne Frank* and *Godspell*. By that point in the season, a number of players had done so many shows together, they had developed a close-knit ensemble and the productions reflected that unity. Maggie was cast as Anne's older sister, Margot, in *Diary* and she was also cast in *Godspell*. Chris had, by this season, decided he preferred the unseen job of stage electrics, and he ran the lights for most of the shows that season. He was surprised, however, to find that *Godspell* would have no walls to hide the techs and he would have to be in costume. While in costume, the director, Mark Swezey, insisted that Chris also be blocked into the ensemble numbers. Larry Pressgrove played the Jesus character. It was to be one of the highlights of the Vassar productions, and a successful run, artistically and financially. The houses were consistently high during the two-week run.

Maggie Rogers and Larry Pressgrove front and center among the cast members of *Godspell* 1979. Chris is far left in the back.

Following the end of the summer, Christopher joined the Pennsylvania Stage Company in Allentown, Pennsylvania as an intern in stage electrics, and Margaret returned to Emporia State University as a junior.

Rick also returned to his home in California, but his cat, Big Kitty, had come to love the country living at Vassar Playhouse. Veda talked Rick into letting Big Kitty stay.

By mid-September Bruce and Veda knew they would have to pare down the staff on the Shortline. The crowds dropped off as the season at the barn ended. They still had pretty good crowds for Saturday nights, and for the Sunday brunch, but daily luncheons and the other evening meals brought in virtually no one. The prices were higher than the other area restaurants, they acknowledged, but the fare was also different from anything offered by other local dining establishments. They did not offer fast food; it was leisure dining and they billed it as "Dining for a special occasion." They hoped that their corner might become, as one customer put it, "The perfect place to become engaged." Or, just to celebrate any special occasion.

They decided to offer special holiday parties for the Christmas season and they sent out their plans to area manufacturers and businesses. This effort resulted in some events for the winter season, but it was still low.

They didn't know whether they could hold on long enough for interest in the train to grow. They couldn't project how long that would take.

Special meals were planned for the holiday parties and they contacted a young couple from Lyndon to help them with the entertainment. Kristi Willhite was the music teacher in Lyndon and she and her husband, Michael, were expecting their first child. The foursome put together several madrigals, with Kristi on top, Veda singing alto, Bruce, tenor, and Michael, bass. The evening would begin in the parlor car where a big vat of wassail steamed on the Franklin stove. As the guests gathered, they would visit over a cup of wassail, and the singers would carol. They had the evening planned with certain Christmas madrigals during the meal which began with them singing "The Boar's Head Carol" as the kitchen staff and crew came behind the quartet bearing a steaming stuffed pig on a platter.

They created a really special Christmas party for a firm or office, but this was in rural Osage County, Kansas, after all, and most area firms were not interested in (1) spending the money assessed for the evening; or (2) taking their employees to the country to celebrate. Thus, their efforts were not very profitable.

Also, in the fall they had been approached by the Kansas Arts Commission to apply for a grant to tour plays for adult audiences. They explained that Vassar Playhouse was a for-profit organization and were told that, in order to be eligible for any grants, it would have to be not-for-profit. They considered the possibility, and after visiting with their children, Bruce and Veda decided to establish a not-for-profit corporation in memory of their daughter. In January 1980 they set up the *Kathryn Rogers Foundation for Artists*. The plan was to begin with theater and grow to support different artists of other genres. The prospect was exciting for them.

They contacted their friends, John and Carole, and Carole agreed to serve as President of the organization. They also met with their long-time friend, Yvonne Eckert, who said she would serve on the board and compose the initial letter that would be mailed to potential donors in the spring. Veda met with the Kansas Arts Commission and applied for grants to enable them to hire a director and pay for a business manager.

They met with and hired Roger Moon as the Artistic Director. Roger previously had a brief stint at the Playhouse in 1973, when he filled in as the title role in the fateful production of *Charlie Brown*. By 1980 he was working on his graduate degree in theater at Emporia State University, and was married to Allyson, a talented actress and director, who had that December given birth to their second son, Garth. They both agreed to move to Vassar the end of May and make the red trailer their family home. Allyson's mother, Betty Stark, was also hired as costumer. She purchased a house in Lyndon and moved into the area. Roger also hired a designer for the season, Rick Tyler, who was on the faculty of McPherson College. The summer season was set. The opening show was to be a double bill, Leonard Bernstein's short opera, *Trouble in Tahiti*, with Bruce and Veda in the roles of Dinah and Sam, and a funny little pastiche based on the 1920's newspaper column of Don Marquis, *archy and mehitabel*. Both of those shows were planned for touring in the fall. Completing the summer fare would be *The King and I*, *The Miracle Worker*, *HMS Pinafore*, *Bus Stop* and *A Little Night Music*, the musical by Stephen Sondheim, which was also planned for touring. Wayne Cherveny was hired to obtain bookings for the fall and winter tours. Grants were obtained for the director and business manager, and the new organization was off.

Chapter Nineteen

The phone rang and four-year old Geoffrey ran to pick it up.
"Hello?" his voice, mature for his age, responded.
"May I please speak to Roger Moon?" The voice on the other end asked.
"Well, Roger isn't here right now." Geoffrey answered.
"Could you give him a message?"
"Of course, let me get a pencil." Geoffrey found a pencil. "What would you like me to tell him?"
"Would you ask him to call Dennis Lickteig?"
"Of course, what is your number, Dennis?"
"My number is 242-3126." The caller answered.
"Just a minute, 2 . . . 4 . . ." And there was a pause, before he resumed, "Excuse me, Dennis, could you please tell me something?"
"Yes, what is it?"
"Could you please tell me how to make a 2?" Geoffrey was four going on forty!

He and his little brother, Garth, were the joys of the season. Roger would carry the baby in a pouch that he wore, and the babe would sleep through the rehearsals and Roger's jumping up from his seat to explain a direction, or seemingly, any noise or interruption. His parents had been toting him to rehearsals since birth and he was totally unaware of anything unusual.

At six months, he was the littlest prince in *The King and I*. Karla Cherveny, who had first appeared at Vassar in 1977 in the role of Winthrop in *The Music Man*, returned the summer of 1980 as a young teenager, appearing in both *King and I* and *The Miracle Worker*, and she assumed the role of taking care of Garth during the performances of the show with many children!

The temperatures were unseasonably hot during the run of *The King and I*, and the players were not without casualty during that run. One evening, just before going on in her heavy velvet traveling suit as Anna Leonowens, Susie Cravens was discovered passed out in the shop behind the stage. The shop, constructed on the back of the barn in 1978, was used for backstage area, as well as for building the set. Susie was revived by rubbing some ice on her face, and a drink of water. Susie, seemingly recovered, then made her way to the stage and sang with usual gusto her rendition of *Whistle a Happy Tune*.

Earlier in the spring, the owners had purchased a compartment car, Regal Ruby, which sat on the siding where the former chicken house had stood. It was their plan to air condition the *Ruby*, but due to various delays, the players still slept in the heat until the first of July. By the end of June, they had already logged several ninety-degree evenings, and it was also very dry. It was a wonder any of the cast stayed around before they were finally given air cooled quarters.

The temperatures for the next show *The Miracle Worker* gave no better comfort. Bill Christie was there that summer of 1980. He managed the box office and logged the evening statistics with the house count, the gate receipts, concessions, and the temperature at curtain time, 8:17 PM. His log for the summer showed four weeks straight with temperatures in the upper nineties or higher. Finally, on July 22nd, during *Miracle Worker* when the temperature dropped to 85 degrees, he wrote "Splendiloquent!" That was not the end of the hot spell, but it did begin to ease somewhat.

Bruce had directed *A Little Night Music* for the Winfield Community Theater in the fall of 1975. He asked the musicians from that production if they would be willing to make a tape to provide the orchestra and ensemble for the fall Vassar production. They all agreed, and in mid-July Veda made the trip to spend several days in Winfield while they rehearsed and cut the tape. She had arranged to use the Winfield High School's recording studio and they hired a recording technician from Wichita to do the mixing. It was her first experience of that type endeavor. She rehearsed the orchestra most of the day and brought in the Liebeslieder singers toward evening. They rehearsed and were soon ready to begin recording. Veda wanted to begin with the instrumental ensemble and said she would call the singers in when she was ready for them. The session was long and arduous. It was well after midnight before they even began to record the vocal ensemble, and dawn was breaking before they were finished. She thanked everyone for their good and hard work and made the tired journey back to Vassar. It was several weeks before the technician had the master and performance copies ready.

Life's About a Dream

A Little Night Music 1980. L-R: Veda, Julie Kriekhaus, Allyson Moon, Kristi Willhite, Bruce, and Susie Cravens.

The couple also wanted to acquire a winter performance space for the company of actors and they met with the directors for the Vassar Community Building, the former elementary school in Vassar. They negotiated a lease for the winter, agreeing to free up the building for any special events the board had planned, and also, giving them the schedule of the days and evenings the troupe would request its use for rehearsal or performance. It was a small space, one level and very intimate. The artistic staff decided to perform plays in the round and they set about creating a season for the winter months which included *Arms and the Man, Who's Afraid of Virginia Wolf?, All My Sons, Miss Julie, California Suite, Much Ado about Nothing,* an original review entitled *acting 101,* and ending the season with the Jones and Schmidt musical *Philemon.*

The permanent acting company for that first year of the Kathryn Rogers Foundation for Artists included Tim Counts, Miles Norton, Susie Cravens, Julie Krieckhaus, Lenette Steinle, Bill Christie, Allyson Moon and Ron Freeby. Allyson's mother, Betty Stark, was the costumer and Rick Tyler from McPherson College was hired as the set designer with Roger Moon as artistic director. Additional players for the summer season included Andy Garrison, Diana Gish, Dennis Lickteig, Bill Ellwood, Jim Bowles, Susan Carson and Karla Reisch. Eleanor Richardson and Wayne Cherveny came in for special appearances in *Bus Stop*, and Kristi Willhite and Carolyn Crowell were brought in to complete the cast of *Night Music*. Brian Larios, a student from Ottawa, was cast as Rafe Rakestraw in *HMS Pinafore*.

The schedule for the winter months was as intense as for the summer, although the performance week at the schoolhouse was shortened to four nights. The owners believed they were fulfilling the purpose of the not-for-profit foundation by providing a place for the actors and theater technicians to practice and hone their craft. During that first year, Tim Counts, who was cast in all of the shows except *Tahiti*, played eleven major roles in the same number of months. There was probably not a theater in the United States that was providing any more experience for an actor. And the shows were artistically well planned and rehearsed; they were not just "slapped together." Roger paid diligent attention to the quality of performance and the appropriate development of each character. He was almost religious in that effort, to the point of exhaustion following the opening of most shows. He would often stay up all night toward the end of the rehearsal and building process. In fact, Bruce and Veda found that trait to be his one flaw. He couldn't seem to pace his energies. Once a show got opened, Roger would nearly always be in bed with a migraine headache for a couple of days. He truly suffered.

Chris had returned from his year with the Pennsylvania Stage Company in Allentown, Pennsylvania, before the season began in May. He had first thought he would stay with the company and work tech for the opening show. He later decided, however, to move to Wichita during the summer to live with his friend, Victor. He planned to get a job and enroll at Wichita State University for the coming school year. His parents supported the decision and he left the Playhouse that summer.

Maggie had also decided against returning to Vassar that summer, her first year away from her summer home, and she entered the summer program at Emporia State University. Too, she had that spring discovered the first love of her life, David Young, and the bug had hit her hard. The parents had met David a couple of times; Maggie and David had appeared together in several shows at ESU. They liked him, but they didn't know him. "But," as her mother said, "we trust you to make your own decision and know what you are doing. We love you all the same!"

* * *

Meanwhile, during the past two years, Veda and Bruce had numerous meetings with attorneys in regard to the Whippoorwill lawsuits. They attended many depositions and even more routine meetings. Each meeting would hold many lawyers representing all of the defendants which included the Lighthouse Bay Marina, Kansas Department of Parks and Recreation, the State of Kansas, the Osage County Sheriff's Department, the Kansas Fish and Game Commission, the Kansas Steamboat Company (Bill Hurtig et al who had constructed the boat), the Leavenworth Steel Works (they built the hull) and other entities long forgotten. There was never a meeting with less than ten lawyers present. Bruce and Veda felt very transparent in the sessions. The talk was always what the "game plan" would be, the tactics to use, the arguments to present. There never seemed to be a search for truth or justice. The couple felt they had done nothing wrong; they had followed their usual procedures that fateful evening. How could it be construed that there was negligence on their part, or on the part of anyone else?

And they would, from time to time, receive transcripts of the depositions for them to read. Volumes. It was all painful reading, but they had to get through it to ensure the recorder had been accurate about what they said. Bruce often asked the lawyers who would pay for his interruption of work to attend the many meetings. "Why can I not expect some restitution for my pain? Are we nobody?"

His cousin, James Logan, was the lead spokesman for the marina. He looked at Bruce vaguely at first, then warmed to respond, "You know, Bruce, we attorneys do sometimes forget the clients, and they are the real issue in the case." Yet he had no ready answer for Bruce.

Veda felt even less visible than her husband, because she hadn't been on the boat. She was at the Playhouse when the storm hit and, although she was expected to attend the meetings, she was never given the opportunity to say her piece. And she had plenty to say: she wanted to remind them that Bruce had studied weather when he was a navigator with the US Air Force, that he had indeed checked the weather before starting out that evening—he had not only visibly checked, but he also consulted the US Weather Service. She wanted to remind them that the radio had been on where she was working and, in accordance with the station's usual procedure when a potential storm was afoot, there was not the periodic beep of weather warning with their broadcast. But she never got the chance. The more she thought about those meetings, the more upsetting it was.

During their "winter of discontent," when they were working to restore the train, a reporter from Wichita had asked to interview them for the Wichita Eagle. The couple allowed him to come. They tried to keep the interview positive, showing him their plans for the train, but he kept coming back to the darker topics of the previous summer's tragedy and the ensuing death of their daughter in the fall. "How are you feeling about everything at this point? I imagine you want to find someone to take the blame, don't you?"

"Whom can we blame? The storm that hit the Whippoorwill came out of the blue without warning. The doctors, too, have been unable to explain Kathryn's illness. It came without warning. Who is there? And what good would it do us, if we had someone to blame?"

They had by that point received the autopsy report with Dr. Kaufman's notes attached. The examiner had found nothing out of the ordinary in Kate's condition except fluid in her lungs, which the doctor explained was a normal occurrence at the end of life.

"Do you want to take the responsibility?" Veda asked the reporter.

"You folks must have a great deal of faith." He responded.

"I don't think it is any greater than anyone I know. We are normal grieving parents who long to rediscover our formerly normal lives. We're still alive and must continue, so we are forging our energies into the project which was begun months before the Whippoorwill tragedy. And we will continue the summer plays that we have been producing for the past nine years."

The reporter then took some photos. Bruce and Veda always dreaded a photographer's shots of the Playhouse during the off-season. Everything looked bleak and dreary. They reminded him, "Come back in the summer when we are teeming with customers before you publish your article." But, of course, he didn't.

Chapter Twenty

Mimi was always a favorite with the summer players. She would make many appearances at the playhouse, day or night, often bringing her little dachshund, Twiggy, with her. But, by the summer of 1979 everyone could tell she was failing. During the run of *Sound of Music*, Veda's 12-year old niece, Sara, who was in the cast as one of the children, was staying in Quenemo with Grandmother Driver. One evening Mimi was driving Sara home after performance and, as Sara later related,

"She drove past her house in Quenemo and just kept on going. We were in the country somewhere and I said something to her. She said she didn't know where she was. Somehow, she got the car turned around and headed back the other direction. We reached Quenemo and then, she took me on up to Grandma's." Incidents such as this were beginning to happen more and more frequently.

She continued to live by herself in the family home in Quenemo, but Bruce or Veda or both would check on her daily, sometimes making several trips before a day was done. In the fall of 1979, the couple decided to take her to WaKeeney to visit her cousins in Western Kansas before winter set in. They made the brief trip over the weekend of October 2nd, the day that would have been Kate's 21st birthday. All of the books had said that holidays and birthdays are always the hardest to endure after the loss of a loved one.

Mimi was like a child on the trip with her questions. "How much longer 'til we get there? Who are we going to see? Now, just what relation is she?"

It was obvious to the couple that her dementia was getting worse. And she was periodically surly and bad tempered. It was a growing concern for the couple wondering what they were going to do, and knowing that a decision would have to be made very soon. Seeing her with her relatives and long ago friends in WaKeeney was also difficult for the couple. She would often repeat herself or ask the same question over and over.

"Now, Myrt, I've already told you about that!" Her favorite cousin Nora wouldn't allow her to ask more than once.

"I know, but what did you say?" And Myrtle would ask again.

It was comical, and at the same time sad, but the couple was very glad they had made the trip for Mimi. She would not likely ever see her cousins again.

A year later, following the Christmas holidays of 1980, the company was furloughed for a few weeks, and Bruce and Veda arranged to spend a week at the Gibson cabin in Green Mountain Falls, Colorado, with Maggie and Chris. They had always found a sense of peace in the mountain valley along U.S. 24 and that week would prove no exception.

Before their departure they made arrangements for a friend to look in on Mimi at her house and take her places so she wouldn't wonder "Where are the kids?"

Upon their return and after their children had returned to school, they decided to purchase a mobile home to set on the concrete slab that had once been a garage, and move Mimi out to the Playhouse with them. They went into Ottawa and made the purchase before they changed their minds. Then, they went into Quenemo to visit with Mimi.

She wept quietly, truly realizing what her son was asking her to do.

"I have lived here over 50 years—I don't want to leave my own house."

And Bruce came into the dining room where Veda was seated at the table putting together a jigsaw puzzle. "I can't do it, Veda. She understands what is happening."

"Of course, she understands now, but Bruce, you know that you cannot allow her to live by herself any longer. It isn't safe for her and we all know her driving is not safe for her passengers."

Her unpredictable mood swings and actions had literally chased her *former* friends away. She had only a couple who realized, "This is not the Myrtle we have known and loved."

He continued to press his mother. "Mimi, we will try it for awhile. We won't sell your house; and if you are terribly unhappy with us, we can bring you back to Quenemo." That promise worked, and she moved to the Playhouse a few weeks later, in January 1981.

It was convenient having her at the Playhouse. Bruce took her car keys out of her purse, but he parked the car next to the new mobile home, and when she felt she needed more independence, the couple would find her seated behind the wheel of her car. She would sit there for awhile and then, come back into the house, evidently satisfied that her means of escape was still within reach, should she decide to use it.

Old friends began to stop to see Mimi when they would come to a show. It was fun to watch her puff up as she would boast, "Oh yes, I'm living at Vassar Playhouse now." And upon the first greeting of an old friend, her eyes would light up and she would remember him or her. It was as if nothing were wrong. It would be only a few minutes of visiting, however, when dementia would take over and her friends would know that "Myrtle isn't the same anymore, is she?"

Veda had thought that Mimi would enjoy the children, Geoffrey and Garth Moon, at the Playhouse, but she was mistaken. She didn't respond as much to the little ones as she did to the players. She would just sparkle when any of them came into the mobile home for something. A favorite of hers was Ron Freeby, and he loved Mimi, too. When he would come to see her, she would blush. One evening Ron confided to Veda, "I think Mimi thinks I am her gentleman caller."

Her moods were changing, too. She began to think that Bruce was her husband, and one time Veda overheard her telling a friend that she (Veda) was "That whore who's sleeping with my husband!" At another time, when Veda was helping her mother-in-law with her bath, Mimi patted Veda's hand and said, "You're just the best sister a girl ever had!"

Life at Vassar became a challenge for involving Mimi, and keeping her busy without giving her too much access to the customers. She would pull them aside and tell them stories, too. And, of course, they believed her—for awhile.

By the summer of 1981, however, she seemed pretty content to stay at home with the air conditioning during the day and walk over to the barn or train in the evenings. Roger and Allyson directed the shows that season, opening with *The Glass Menagerie* with Veda and Allyson in the roles of Amanda and Laura Wingfield. Following that production were *Grease, Our Town, My Fair Lady, Ten Little Indians* and *The Robber Bridegroom.*

The Ascot Races *My Fair Lady* 1981. L-R: Judy Ney, Miles Norton, Jan Zabel Susie Cravens, Chris King, Dennis Lickteig, Wendy Parman, Allyson Moon, Tim Counts, Kevin Barrett and Gretchen Kehde. (I know I've missed some.)

The temperatures were much more pleasant that season and the audiences began to pick up after *Grease* got underway, but profits were still elusive. Veda and Bruce had managed to pump an additional $80,000 into the operations during 1980, and they didn't have anything else they could do. There were many meetings with Roger to see where spending cuts could be made. He had good arguments, but they had no choice. Roger wasn't going to pay the bills and the couple wouldn't be able to either unless there were drastic measures taken.

Several of the players had remained from the previous year: Tim Counts, Susie Cravens, Dennis Lickteig and Miles Norton. Also returning from an earlier season were Jan Zabel and Hal Bundy who were both involved in the summer of 1979. Newcomers were Greg Baber, Kevin Barrett, Michael Czeranko, Gretchen Kehde, Pam Kerrihard, Chris King, Judy Ney, Wendy Parman, Lisa Lack, Ida Yarborough, Jeri Stanfield and Kevin Shoenhals. Ron Freeby remained to work on the train and Betty Stark and Rick Tyler were costumer and set designer.

In August, Bruce had a request from Ottawa University to fill an interim position in the theater department until the trustees could hire a permanent person. He discussed the position with the University and then, approached Roger with the idea of his doing it. Roger accepted the position. The fall program held a brief tour of *Grease* and a fall season at the Osage City Opera House. The Vassar Community Center had not renewed its lease to use that space for the winter, and Bruce and Veda met with the owners of the Osage City Bowling Alley, who also owned the space above them which was the original Osage City Opera House. They felt it would work very nicely for a season. They were still open for lunch and dinner on the train, with a Sunday brunch. They offered a special deal on the train with a show at the opera house ten miles away.

They scheduled *Barefoot in the Park* to open the fall season to be followed by the Jones and Schmidt musical *Celebration*. Although the dinners and show in two separate places appeared to work the previous year, it was just too far between the train and Osage City to be feasible. The couple soon realized they had to make more drastic changes. Early in November, when they were into the opening week of *Celebration*, Bruce and Veda assembled the cast and announced they would have to release them. They had made the decision to continue at the Opera House with a bare bones crew. The December show would be changed to *I Do! I Do!*, with Bruce and Veda performing the roles, and anyone who wished to stay to help were welcome, but they would not be able to pay them the wages they had been earning. Ron Freeby was still working with them. He had that summer moved into Mimi's house in Quenemo. He wanted to stay and help. Tim and Miles also offered to stay.

After two years of working with the talented cast, the decision to stop was very difficult for everyone. The couple had enjoyed their company and felt they fulfilled the original purpose of the Kathryn Rogers Foundation. When a customer would chance to talk to them for a while after a show, they would always conclude any conversation with, "I'll bet you have a lot of fun." Little did they realize the work, the number of hours a play took to put on stage, but yes, they did have fun, too. For Bruce's birthday that fall, for instance, the cast treated him to a surprise party at Hazel's, a strip bar just down the road east from the Playhouse. Hazel was a 50 something bleached blonde slip of a woman who lived in Vassar and always wore wedgies, mules. Some years before, she and her husband had established a bar at the entrance to the dam. Just a bar with a pool table and some booths, it was the *Red Fox*. The players had hung out at the Red Fox since 1970. When she and her husband divorced, Hazel wound up with the house in Vassar and the bar. In recent years, hoping to spice it up a bit, she had begun hiring topless dancers from Topeka and her place had become *notorious* among the locals.

The cast arranged on the sly with Veda to get Bruce to Hazel's after the show on September 4th. So that night, needing to stall a bit, she suggested they take a drive. That wasn't an unusual request, but when she said, "No, I'll drive!" he began to suspect something was up. They drove to the dam and on down to one of their favorite spots for star gazing. Veda stopped the car and, as Bruce started to get out, she said,

"No, I've changed my mind. I want to go somewhere else." And they got into the car and drove back across the dam. She pulled into Hazel's parking lot.

"What are we doing here?" He questioned her several times.

"Well, if you will try a little patience, maybe you'll find out!"

They walked into the bar, a first time for either of them.

"SURPRISE!" The cast all sang Happy Birthday to Bruce.

Suzie Cravens told him, "We've talked to Hazel and she is going to have the stripper do a special number for you, Bruce."

Bruce started to blush. They all ordered a beer and began talking about the evening's performance of *Robber Bridegroom*. They were there only a few minutes when an argument between two men, "Rednecks," Tim called them, developed at the bar. Music was playing and the dancer was doing her thing, but before they knew what was happening, a sheriff's car pulled up with lights flashing and a deputy came into the establishment.

"It's a raid!" Miles slapped his knee and shouted.

The deputy sheriff announced, "Okay, everyone just get into your cars and go quietly to your homes."

"What is going on?" Bruce thought this was all part of his surprise party. He was pushed to the door along with the others.

Then, as Hazel turned out the lights and locked the door behind her, she came over to Bruce and said,

"I am so sorry. One of those men was pickin' for a fight, and I don't put up with any of that shit. You come to my place, you behave!" And she apologized,

"My girl didn't get to do her special dance for you. I hope you are not too disappointed."

Bruce assured her he would be all right. As they walked to their cars, he waved to the sheriff and then called to the players,

"Hey thanks for the best birthday party I've ever had."

*   *   *

So, in December they closed the train for the winter, except for the kitchen car, where the meals were prepared; and they began catering dinners to the Osage City Opera House. It wasn't a lucrative operation, but they could survive.

Tim and Miles stayed through the run of *I Do! I Do!*, then leaving for Minneapolis. During their fifteen months at Vassar, both young men had been involved one way or another in some twenty-five different productions, many of which were major roles. Tim left saying he felt burned out. He thought he wouldn't do theater for a while!

I Do! I Do! closed in January and the next play was *Sleuth*, with Charley Oldfather, who drove in from Lawrence, and Chris Waugh, from Topeka. Next they scheduled a review, *Tintypes*, which the trio (Bruce, Veda and Ron) performed with two other young actors from the community.

They next performed two one acts by Anthony Shaffer, *The Private Ear* and *The Public Eye*, which actually opened "on the road." A tour of *Grease* had been scheduled for the spring of 1982, and the company was to perform in Augusta and Junction City, where a second show had been scheduled, as well. The cast of the earlier tour had dispersed. Bruce and Veda contacted all who could return and then, they called Jim Olson who was studying at KU and asked him to perform the role of Danny Zuko. He was eager to and asked, "Do you need any more players?"

"As a matter of fact we do." Bruce recited the roles he needed to fill. Jim filled all of them with KU players who had performed in their production of the show or who were just eager to act. They came to Vassar on two different weekends, working one whole day at the Vassar Community Center, which had been arranged for a one-day rehearsal; and spending another cold day on the stage of the barn. Veda served as director and also played the piano for that show. She took notes and rehearsed all that they could in the short time frame allowed; and then, during the week she wrote the cast long letters with her notes. They teased her about "directing by correspondence." But it worked.

The run of *Grease* at the playhouse during the summer had included an ASL signer for the hearing impaired. In fact, Vassar Playhouse was one of the first theatres in Kansas to offer signed productions for the hearing impaired and they did that for at least two productions: *The Miracle Worker* and *Grease*. David Lawrence, from Kansas City, Kansas, was born to deaf parents and had been signing all his life. He was able to *act* the songs and dances, taking part at times, as well as interpreting the dialogue. He went along on the tour, too. The other returning players in that cast were Dennis Lickteig, Ron Freeby, Chris King, and Pam Kerrihard. Veda, Hal Bundy and a drummer provided orchestra. The new members, which Jim Olson had drafted from KU were, besides Jim: Wendy Hildyard, Gail Bronfman, Lisa (Kessinger) Divel, Brad Zimmerman, Dwight Dickey, LeWan Alexander, and Cathy Barnett.

Poor Mimi, however, was so confused. She had become progressively worse through that winter. In fact, when Bruce had her hospitalized for tests in January, she gave the hospital staff such a hard time that the doctor said as he released her, "We must, at any cost, keep your mother out of the hospital!" Physically she seemed well, but mentally her dementia was taking over.

When she received word of the death of Bruce's cousin, Louise Logan Eagle, Mimi's mind was focused and obsessed upon her longtime friend. She wanted to go to the funeral. Bruce said he would take her when it was time. Thus, when Mimi heard singing coming from the barn, she donned her coat, hat and warm gloves and made her way to the theater where she sat in the center of the fourth row and watched the gyrations of the cast as they rehearsed the energetic dance numbers for *Grease*. After several numbers, Bruce left the kitchen car where he had been working and joined his mother. She huddled next to him and said confidentially,

"I hope you don't hold one of these for me when I die!"

Later when he was telling Veda about it, Bruce laughed, "I think she evidently thought she was at Louise's funeral!"

Life's About a Dream

Grease Tour Spring 1983. Front L-R: Chris King, Wendy Hildyard, LeWan Alexander, Cathy Barnett and Dennis Lickteig. 2nd Row: David Lawrence, Gail Bronfman, Dwight Dickey, Lisa Divel, Ron Freeby and Brad Zimmerman. On top are Pam Kerrihard and Jim Olson.

The company had toured *Grease* the previous fall (with different cast members, of course) to the city of Concordia, where they played the historic Brown Grand Opera House. They had previously played there in 1980 with their tour of *Night Music*. For the *Grease* tour, Pam Kerrihard, who played Sandy in the summer production, had been unavailable for that fall tour, and the company brought in Kristi Willhite from Lyndon who had also been in *Night Music* the year before. The performance went well and as the final curtain fell, she gave her cohort, Tim Counts, a hug before falling off a platform injuring her leg. She was hospitalized and it was several weeks before she was able to fully use her limb. By the following spring Pam was once again available, so the tour was planned with her back in the role.

Bruce and Veda arranged for a caretaker for Mimi before they left on tour. They would be gone only five days, but they couldn't leave Mimi by herself. They had already had enough scares to know she couldn't be left alone. One early morning, for instance, Bruce awakened to the smell of smoke and got up to find his mother sitting at the kitchen table while an empty plastic dish was on fire in the broiler. "Mimi, what are you doing?"

"Oh, I am just sitting here waiting for you to get up, so I can have my breakfast."

He scurried to the range turning off the oven. "Did you put this in the broiler?"

"No, I don't know *who* did that." It was about 3:00 a.m. and it was unlikely they'd had visitors during the night. The couple realized they needed help.

* * *

The troupe packed up the truck with the set for *Grease*. Bruce, Ron and Lisa Kessinger Divel had been rehearsing during their "spare" time on the next show for the Opera House, the double bill by Anthony Shaffer, *The Private Ear* and *The Public Eye*. It wasn't ready, but they planned to finish it during their off hours between shows in Junction City where they would perform it at the Junction City Little Theatre.

Before closing the door to the truck, Ron called to Bruce, "Shall I take this along?" as he displayed a piece of fabric.

"Yeah, throw it on the truck."

"What about these?" And Ron held up some tapestries that had been painted for *The Sound of Music* in 1979.

"Sure, why not?" It went like that for several minutes as Ron would find something in the properties car, the costume room or wherever. After they had finally tossed what they felt would be sufficient on the truck, the cast and crew set off for Augusta, the first stop. They were scheduled to meet with a group of students in the afternoon and perform the show in its entirety in the evening.

The next morning, the truck set out for Junction City, while the players all returned to their schools. They would not perform again until Saturday, but Ron and Bruce planned to work on the Shaffer one-acts and get that set built for a Friday evening performance. They arrived at the Junction City Little Theater before noon and were heartily welcomed by the person who had been appointed to meet the traveling troupe of players. "When do the actors arrive?" The young man was an enthusiastic "wanna be."

Ron responded, "Oh, they'll come along later."

Afterward he and Bruce laughed, "What do you mean, where are the actors? WE ARE IT!" And they began to assemble the pieces which they had brought with them from the storage cars at Vassar.

Meanwhile, Veda was on a quest for a recording of Benjamin Britten's *Peter Grimes,* which provided essential sound cues for the Shaffer script. She went to K-State and, with the help of someone in their theater department, found the appropriate recording and made the tape. She was appointed to run the sound and lights for the show. What a funny farce. Lisa and the fourth cast member, Bart Ewing, who came in from KU, joined them for a rehearsal that evening. There were, of course, some persons from Junction City Little Theatre on hand. Bruce tried everything he could to talk them into leaving, so as to hold a private rehearsal, but they stayed. One gentleman seemed to have possession of the light booth and was determined to run the lights whether he knew the show or not. Veda battled with him to let her run the board. She knew the show better and it would be much easier to run than to call the cues. Her game plan, in fact, was to wait for a pause and then, *blackout.* There might be a lot of pauses and she wanted to be ready! Even in a slow well-rehearsed process, Bruce was not known for sticking to the script. This particular show would be the challenge of the century for anyone connected to it. It had *not* been a slow, well-rehearsed process, to begin with, and Bruce didn't even have the plot down, let alone the lines. All he knew was if the other person on stage wasn't speaking, it was his turn!

The rehearsal was not good. The set was not finished. The lights were not set. And there were other smaller problems as well. But, rehearsal over, Lisa drove back to her teaching job in Topeka, and Bart drove back for school the next day at KU. Bruce, Veda and Ron stayed to use the next day to put the physical structure together.

The performance was a nightmare for Veda. She didn't feel it was so bad on stage, but she had such a problem with the other person in the booth not letting her run the cues. Phone cues were slow, the doorbell didn't work, lights were slow and it was maddening. She tried to keep a cool head so she could gain control. Finally, for the second one-act, he let her have her way and she felt it went more smoothly. When the final curtain descended, she left the light booth and made her way to the stage where old friends from the theater had begun to congregate to talk to Bruce and Veda. She hugged her husband and started to say something, but before she could open her mouth, he shouted,

"I KNOW! IT WASN'T SO BAD. THE WHIPPOORWILL WAS WORSE!"

Chapter Twenty-One

"What are we going to do for Munchkins?" Ron was asking. He was meeting with Bruce and Veda to discuss preparations for the summer's opening show, *The Wizard of Oz*. Bruce was to direct the 1982 season and the company would be downsized from the two previous seasons.

"We have to keep costs down," Bruce said.

"I've got an idea!" And Veda's eyes began to twinkle with excitement. "How about using puppets?"

"Are you out of your mind?" Her husband asked. "Puppets? How?"

She went on to explain that the cast, or puppeteers, could be hidden behind a black curtain. Bruce and Ron soon caught the excitement and a new and different production of *Wizard* was born. The set was designed to look like a picture book. The costumes were the traditional storybook dress for Dorothy, the tin man, lion and scarecrow. The Munchkins, however, showed up as little puppets, which Ron had created. For the Munchkin scenes the enterprising company made a tape that, while it was recorded in a low voice and slow speed, it was played at a faster rate pushing the tempo up to normal and raising the key an octave. The result gave the fairytale characters the high-pitched tone of the original movie version of Frank Baum's tale. In performance Veda was able to play the piano live for the real actors and then, cue up the tape and push the sound button for the little Munchkins. It worked! In fact, the result was delightful.

The cast for that season included Laure Ronnebaum who, showing up for work early before the summer began, reported to the yellow trailer dressed to the nines and Veda asked,

"Do you plan to wear those high heels?"

"Oh, I am able to work in them just fine," Laure responded. She had worked several summers in a shoe store in her hometown of Olathe and owned a wardrobe of beautiful shoes.

Veda, on the other hand, was dressed in her usual cutoff jeans and sneakers, wearing no makeup and already sweating with the early summer heat.

"We don't expect you to maintain appearances offstage unless you are doing a promo in Topeka or Ottawa. Here you will need to run across the gravel parking lot and up and down the rock house stairs several times a day. We encourage you to dress so as to make the work tolerable."

After her first day as costumer in the sweatshop, Laure learned the wisdom of Veda's words. She never again tried to walk across the crushed rock in her high heels.

Laure was cast in the ingénue roles that summer, Dorothy in *Wizard*, Julie Jordan in *Carousel* and Mabel in *Pirates of Penzance*. Other cast members included, besides Ron Freeby: Paul Soule, Scott Lynes, Aaron Gragg, Marla Wiens, Kraig Kerger, Lori Bryant, Leslie Casson, Nancy Bevensee, Karen Kotas and David Atchison. The 1982 schedule also included *Da* and *You Can't Take it With You*. A young couple from Ottawa, Nick and Jeanette George, joined the company for *You Can't Take it With You* and stayed through the fall and winter season. Kristi Willhite was brought in to play Carrie Pipperidge in *Carousel*.

Mimi's dementia was almost complete by the time the summer began. Bruce and Veda hired a young woman from Vassar to stay with her during the day. The young mother would bring her baby boy with her and they would provide companionship and care for Mimi. The art of conversation, even the ability to speak, had left the ailing woman. One evening early in the summer, Veda had walked Mimi to the barn and was sitting with her in the old porch swing which Bruce had installed on the patio. They were swinging lazily when Paul Soule walked up. Veda asked her mother-in-law,

"Mimi, do you remember when we lived in Winfield?" And Mimi nodded.

"Do you remember our minister at the Presbyterian Church, Rev. Soule?" Again Mimi nodded her head. Veda continued, "Well, this is his son, Paul."

And Mimi's eyes sparkled as she smiled at Paul and tried to say she was glad to see him again. Her periods of lucidity came so infrequently by this time that they became moments to treasure. More often her communication skills would take other forms. One time the couple returned to their mobile home to find a message from Mimi written on an emery board. Another time when she was still able to speak but words were hard to form, Bruce showed her a picture of his father with his two brothers, Bruce and Fred. Bruce said to Mimi, "Do you know who these fellows are?" She nodded.

"Who are they, Mimi?"

"Well, that is—" (pause) and she pointed to Bruce's Uncle Fred, "And that is . . . ah . . ." as she pointed to Uncle Bruce. Then she singled out John L. and said confidently, "Of course, I know who this is! That's . . . ." And then, after a long pause, "Well, anyway, I'll never forget ole' what's his name."

Mimi's special beau was Ron Freeby, and he was cast in the title role of *Da* with Lori Bryant and Kraig Kerger as his wife and son, Charlie. For the role Ron had bleached his hair white and allowed it to grow longer than normal, as Da is from the Scottish highlands. One evening, Bruce had stayed with his mother until she was asleep and then, he went on to the barn to view the evening show. As he watched one of Da's long soliloquies, he noticed Mimi shuffling down the east aisle barefoot and in her pink pajamas. He loped across the empty back rows to catch her as he whispered, "No, Mimi!" And he gently steered her out of the barn. She had heard her young friend's voice and was just walking down the aisle to see him; that was all.

Every show has its special memories and *Carousel* had more than its share. One evening near the end of the first act, during the *Blow High, Blow Low* sequence, as the actors were marching lock step across the apron of the stage, it happened: Kraig Kerger, as Billy Bigelow, was in step in front of Ron who was playing the role of Jigger. When they all fell at the appointed moment, the knife Ron was wearing in his belt plunged into Kraig's left leg. At the end of the number, Kraig darted into the dressing room where Laure, seeing the gash in his leg, ripped up a petticoat and tied a tourniquet around his leg. He returned to the stage to sing Billy's *Soliloquy* before the first act curtain descended. Meanwhile, Bruce was notified of the accident and telephoned Dr. Adams in Osage City. The doctor agreed to meet him at his office during intermission. The curtain fell and Bruce and Kraig left before the customers descended onto the patio and the cooler night air for their intermission dessert.

Intermission was longer than usual that evening and when the customers became restless, Veda decided she should tell them the reason for the delay. As she was explaining the events that occurred shortly before intermission, the familiar Mazda whizzed into the parking lot and the cast began their second act. Had they not been told, the audience would not have known anything was wrong with the actor playing Billy Bigelow!

It was during *Carousel* that Mimi passed away. Veda sang the role of Nettie Fowler and on Thursday evening, August 5th, during her rendition of *When you Walk Through a Storm*, Mimi awakened with Bruce sitting at her bedside. She didn't speak, but he knew she was awake and totally aware. She knew him, knew where she was and knew it was time. Bruce held his mother and told her he loved her. "It's a beautiful summer evening, Mimi. It's all right." She drew her last breath as he held her very peacefully in his arms. He continued to sit with her until he could hear the audience leaving after the evening's performance. He then calmly walked across the parking lot to tell Veda and the cast. It was Ron who asked, "Can I see her? I was her best beau, you know." And he went to her room to say goodbye.

Veda then asked Lori Bryant if she would step in as Nettie for the weekend. She knew she could probably sing the role, and under most circumstances, she would say the show must go on. "But, I know Mimi would prefer that I stop until after the funeral." They never planned for understudies, but one could always be found when the need arose.

The cast was in rehearsal for *You Can't Take it With You* when Mimi died. Nearing opening day Bruce still needed a policeman for the final scene, and he telephoned Rick Rottschaefer. "How would you like to come finish the summer with us, play the last act policeman in this show and design and direct *Pirates of Penzance*? It worked out for Rick to leave early from his summer position at Nashville's Opryland, and he arrived on opening night just a few hours before he was to go onstage! A trouper knows his entrance.

Bruce and Veda had not worked with Rick since their "winter of discontent" in 1978-1979 and his subsequent years of graduate training were evident with the *Pirates'* first rehearsal. His designs for *Pirates* were delightful and, as Bruce and Veda were to learn when the rehearsal process began, so were his ideas for the show. He found such frivolity in the Gilbert and Sullivan shows and was able to infect the cast with his love of this particular show. He worked well with the small cast and found ways to turn the big fight scenes between the pirates and the policemen into farce. The cast of five males would appear as pirates and then, one by one, run off to change into policemen, back onstage to fight in that role and so on. The cast used to tell audience members, "If you think the show is frantic onstage, you should see it backstage!" Each of the women was assigned to a male, to have his clothes and properties ready when he would dash off for the quick change.

A fall tour had also been scheduled for *Pirates*. Following the summer, the cast left for western Kansas. A customer, Carl Zscheile, from Burlington, always donated a van from his Chevrolet agency for the playhouse tours and this year was no exception. The 12-member "company" drove out in the 9-passenger van and a U-Haul truck that could seat three persons. Veda was a member of the tour, not only in the role of Ruth, but also to handle the expenses of the trip. They played *Pirates* on the road eighteen performances in as many small towns of Western Kansas. It was not always a pleasant experience. Laure Ronnebaum suffered an extreme bout of bronchitis and had to see a doctor in two different towns. She would sleep feverishly during the day and someone would punch her when it was time to get ready for the show. She would then manage to go onstage and lilt Mabel's high notes as if she were in top form. It never ceased to amaze the cast how she could do that.

The music for the show was on tape which had its advantages as well as disadvantages. Taping the music assured consistent tempos, and the singers did adapt quickly. Once they became accustomed to it, they would find they could even play around with their solos within the given constraints. Of course, the disadvantages were the same as the advantages, in that the tempos did not change. The actors had to adapt and make the best use of what was given. From a production standpoint, however, it was a win-win situation, because all of the players could be utilized on stage or on tech and the shows maintained a consistent pace, even after many performances. So, many of the musicals after the Whippoorwill were performed with taped accompaniment. Even the boat, with its generator variations causing tempos and pitch to vary, had been able to use all of its players and crew in some fashion during the brief shows. The sound would be controlled in the pilot house and often, someone would monitor the boiler so the engineer could run up to the top deck to do a number. The owners could never claim that the shows on the boat had a lot of polish, but the talent of the players always shone through the unpredictable glitches of the generator, the insects and the weather. The result was a great time for the passengers and when the owners ceased running the Whippoorwill due to the many lawsuits which came out of the tragedy of June 1978, many persons continued to express their sorrow at its cessation. They liked the leisure cruise, the food, the entertainment, everything.

The Pirates of Penzance 1982. L-R: Lori Bryant, Marla Wiens, Nancy Bevensee, Aaron Gragg, David Atchison, Kraig Kerger, Ron Freeby and Laure Ronnebaum.

So, for *Pirates* the music was taped in order to free up as many players as possible and allow them to perform on stage or in the running crew. The touring company totaled 12: six men, Nick George, Aaron Gragg, Kraig Kerger, David Atchison, Paul Soule and Ron Freeby; and six women, Jeanette George, Marla Wiens, Nancy Bevensee, Lori Bryant, Laure Ronnebaum and Veda. Jeanette ran the lights and, sometimes, sound. Usually, Marla and Veda were able to alternate running the sound cues. It was a tight ship as all Vassar shows were. Everyone had a specific chore offstage as well as on.

It was during the *Pirates* tour, somewhere in western Kansas, that Veda was watching the early evening news, which was focused on the strife in Lebanon and, as she was staring at the screen she heard the announcer say, "—live from the ship, USS Guam." And there was a photo shot of the Guam. She cried out, "My word, that is the ship where Chris is!!" Until that moment the fact that her own son was in the middle of a battle zone had not really registered with her. The rest of that tour found her poring over the papers and watching the news whenever she could, just to somehow keep track of him.

Chris had decided during the spring of 1981 to join the navy and see the world. After spending several weeks in basic training, followed by schooling in electrics in Chicago at Great Lakes, he became an electrician's mate and shipped out of Norfolk, Virginia, on the USS Guam. His sea duty on the Guam took him to the coast of Lebanon (just off Beirut) twice and in between those two tours he went to Grenada! He joined the Navy and saw the world. It was violent!

Maggie was graduated from ESU in May 1981 and just prior to her graduation she learned that she had been awarded an internship in theatre management in London. The program was under the auspices of the Kennedy Center. She moved to London in June 1981, just in time to see the wedding of Prince Charles and Lady Diana. She lived in a 4th floor walkup townhouse near the Interaction Community Center, where she worked with various troupes of players. Tom Stoppard spawned his *Dogg's Hamlet and Macbeth* at Interaction. The pieces were 15-minute versions of the Shakespeare plays acted by the traveling *Professor Dogg's Troupe* which came from that small space, as well. If she thought Vassar was small, she learned there are playing spaces that are even more compact. Many shows would rehearse at the center before opening downtown London. The company for *Noises Off*, for example, held their rehearsals there. Maggie said the guffaws, noise and laughter that came out of those rehearsals were so boisterous that many persons would halt in the hallways just to listen and peer in to learn "What's so funny?"

Maggie and Chris would not return to Vassar, except for holidays, for three years.

Chapter Twenty-Two

During the *Pirates* tour in the fall of 1982, she would call home several times each week to talk to Bruce and one evening he announced, "Our ship has come in!" He had received the first checks from the oil wells on his Mother's family farm. For more than 40 years, various speculators had leased the rights to drill on that property just west of WaKeeney, Kansas, and many holes over the years had come up dry. But, a few days before Mimi died, a letter had come from Champlin Oil stating that their tests had come up with oil! Bruce told Mimi, but he wasn't sure she really understood. Mimi had to sign a paper so that the checks could begin coming in, Bruce also had to sign a paper so that one of the checks could come directly to him. His grandfather had willed one sixth of his property to "Bruce Rogers and other children of Myrtle Schwanbeck Rogers." In actuality, he was the only grandchild, but of course, so long as Mimi lived, she could legally adopt a child. Therefore, he had to prove that there were no other children of Myrtle. With Bruce's help, Mimi was able to sign her paper.

The first two checks (Mimi's 5/6 and Bruce 1/6) totaled over $80,000! It was like an answer to prayers, many, many prayers. The idea of it excited Veda so much that she practically slept with her calculator, figuring how to pay the bills and do bigger and better things! The idea of all that money was wholly consuming. She had read stories of people who had won lotteries and how their lives had changed. "Give it to us—we can handle it!"

The fall and winter schedule for the Osage City Opera House was set to begin with *You're a Good Man, Charlie Brown*, with Ron directing. Ron was also in charge of the set construction and one morning shortly before opening night, while building the set, he was holding a board with one knee while he used the power saw. Before he realized it, the saw had reached his leg. He stopped just before it reached the bone. Already in Osage City, the crew rushed him to Dr. Adams' office where he was stitched and sent home to his parents in Council Grove to recuperate a few days before allowing him to try to keep pace with the daily theater schedule, although the fall and winter schedules were never as frantic as the summer months. Opening night for *Charlie Brown* was performed without the director. He returned to the show by the end of the first week with the decision to avoid power tools.

The couple decided on *Babes in Toyland* for the Christmas season. They also made arrangements to tour it for one weekend to play Topeka's Grand Theater. Little did Bruce and Veda realize the weakness of that show's book. It contains some pretty Victor Herbert tunes; but the story and dialogue resemble a junior high operetta. They re-worked the show a little changing some of the scenes, omitting some, cutting and pasting the rest to try to make more sense. But it was still a bad show. The show is a fantasy with very few honest characters. One scene, for example, calls for killer bears, while another features gypsy dancers. A little far-fetched for the small company, as well as their small audiences, and probably the least favorable theater experiences for the Vassar players.

Chris was able to get Christmas leave that year as did Maggie, and they both came home for the holidays. With their newfound "fortune" Bruce and Veda were able to pay the theater bills and really believe there might be a future for their company. So, for the first time in many years, they decided to take a real vacation. They arranged to take their children to New York to celebrate the New Year and see some shows. Between the four of them they saw some 10-12 plays in six days. They then rented a car and drove down the coast of New Jersey to return Chris to Norfolk, Virginia and the USS Guam. Maggie remained with her parents who drove on to Washington to visit some friends and then, flew to New Orleans to visit another couple before returning to KC and Vassar. It was a memorable two weeks before Maggie flew back to London.

After the holidays, the company reassembled to continue their season at the Opera House. The couple had agreed to revive their production of *I Do! I Do!* and play in the early spring of 1983 at Ottawa and Iola. They also had another booking of *Pirates* set for Ottawa, so rehearsals were many for their local performances as well as the tours. At the opera house they would play *The Odd Couple, Angel Street* and *Sweeney Todd*. Then, they would move back to the Playhouse for a campy version of *Dracula, the Musical?* for which they would bring in some other players. The company changed much during the spring season. Kraig Kerger and David Atchison did not return after Christmas. They had been scheduled to play Sweeney and Anthony in *Sweeney Todd* so that show had to be re-cast. And they also had to be replaced in *Pirates*. Then, in February, following the evening after their final performance of *I Do! I Do!* in Iola, as they were getting out of the truck at Vassar to unload the set, Veda developed severe abdominal cramps. A trip to the doctor next day revealed some fibroid tumors in the uterus and she was in surgery the following week for a hysterectomy. She had originally been cast to play Mrs. Lovett in *Sweeney*, but happily gave up that role to Lori Bryant, who also contacted a friend and fellow actor in Tulsa, Robert Bowe, to play the title role.

Paul Soule as Toby in *Sweeney Todd* Spring 1983.

The company always spent much time in the preparation of a play and that particular production of *Sweeney* was especially good. Margret Fenske, who taught music at Osage City High School, was hired to play keyboard for the show. A very talented woman, singer, seamstress and pianist, her bubbly enthusiasm for rehearsal and performance was a welcome addition to the company and they were to enjoy her wit, good humor and her spirit for several years. Veda recuperated from her surgery to run lights for the show. The catered dinner was appropriately potpie, which always brought a laugh from the patrons after they realized the plot of the show.

Life's About a Dream

Rick Rottschaefer came in for his spring break to play the Pirate King in *Pirates* for the Ottawa tour and he also agreed to return as director the following summer of 1983.

Following the spring tour the company moved back to Vassar Playhouse to prepare a late spring production of the zany *Dracula, the Musical*, which is loosely based on the Bram Stoker novel. Having just come out of *Sweeney Todd*, this show was its antithesis. Full of puns, zany characters and awful musical selections, the cast chose to just have fun, and fun it was. They brought in LeWan Alexander who had played the role of Kenickie in the spring 1982 *Grease* "by correspondence" tour, playing the role of Dracula; Marla Wiens was his love interest, Mina, Paul Soule a crazy lunatic, and Ron Freeby. Scott Lynes, who had practically grown up at Vassar Playhouse, appearing in the first Whippoorwill production in 1974, returning as one of the young newsboys for *Gypsy*, in 1975 and then again for the entire season of 1982, was in drag for his role. The writers, Evans, Orton and Lynn, had pulled out all stops for their show, which had small audiences at Vassar, but it was such fun for the players that it served to warm them all up for the summer. which would open with *Brigadoon*, to be followed by *Streetcar Named Desire*, *Westside Story*, *Wait Until Dark* and the musical based on the Studs Terkel documentary, *Working*. Remaining from the past season were Paul Soule, Ron Freeby, Marla Wiens, Laure Ronnebaum, Lori Bryant, Nancy Bevensee, and Margret Fenske. New to Vassar that season were Ron Meyer, Beth Tucker, Brad Keplar, Lauri Boyd, Ellen Mills, Jim Story, Keith Burns, and Glynis Jones, a high school girl from Lyndon. Glynis was brought out to play the paper boy in *Working* and she traveled with the company for the tour, as well as playing the role at the barn.

Jim Story and Nancy Bevensee in *Brigadoon* 1983.

Designed by Rick, *Brigadoon* featured a bridge upstage left. The show opened with Ron Meyer pushing his cart over that bridge, which was raked so steeply, due to the shallow stage depth, that he had to pull back to keep the cart and himself from careening into the audience. The players dubbed the show "Bridge of Doom," and nightly they wondered which actor would be the one to slip. Eventually, they all did!

Westside Story featured Rick Rottschaefer and Laure Ronnebaum in the leading roles. Both actors possessed strong voices and the Act I finale *Tonight* sequence was always a thrill to watch and hear. The dances were also well done. Ellen Mills, a senior at Ottawa High, who served as an apprentice that season, was studying ballet and she brought some other dancer acquaintances, Lauralyn Bodle, Nancy Cayton and Kevin Predmore in from Lawrence. Their talents were ably used in the choreography and execution of the action of the *Rumble*.

The company received a grant from the Kansas Commission for the Humanities to take *Working* into the workplace and perform sections appropriate to the specific job site. There would then be a discussion led by different educators in the field of humanities. As usual, there were many changes in the cast at the end of the season, for some had to return to school. Joining the company for *Working* were Mark Rector and Randy Baughman and, as already mentioned, Glynis Jones. The show is a series of vignettes depicting persons in various lines of work. There is a housewife, a teacher, a stone mason, truck driver, retired person, construction worker, mill worker, a waitress and even a prostitute. It is based on interviews conducted by the Chicago journalist, Studs Terkel. Various composers set the interviews to music and a show was compiled. It worked very well in different formats. For instance, when the company performed in a foundry in Coffeyville, they extracted the sections pertaining to the steel worker, factory worker, etc. and the result was something that related and would be of interest to the workers in that particular site. The tour took the company all over Kansas performing in various worksites. Sometimes they would perform the show in its entirety on a stage.

They also carried a second show on that tour, the Rodgers and Hart camp musical, *The Boys from Syracuse,* based on Shakespeare's *A Comedy of Errors.* Whereas *Working* had a more serious tone, this show was pure farce and fun for the company. Marla Wiens was in the chorus as a courtesan, Laure Ronnebaum, Lauri Boyd, Paul Soule and Mark Rector played the two pairs of young lovers. Veda, in the role of the domineering wife of Dromio, played by Bruce, wore a "fat suit" with enormous bosoms and she sang her role `a la Ethel Merman. The company had played the Concordia Brown Grand Opera House two previous seasons (*Night Music* and *Grease*) and the audience recognized Veda as soon as she hit the stage. When she began belting her first song, the audience howled. Ron played the counterpart of Bruce and Rick played the lost twins' father in chains. For one of the numbers, he choreographed the entire cast in a tap dance sequence—with him entering from the wings tapping (in chains). The production had a lot of "shtick" which many audiences (and maybe even some of the cast) never really understood or appreciated, but it was pure fun for Bruce, Rick and Veda.

Chapter Twenty-Three

When the fall tour of 1983 ended, Veda and Bruce made arrangements to go to Europe to spend Christmas with Maggie who was still in London. Chris was still on the USS Guam in the Mediterranean off the coast of Beirut and would be unable to get away for the holidays. The couple set aside six weeks to spend overseas, approximately three weeks in London, two weeks on a train tour through Germany on a Eurorail Pass and one week in Paris visiting their French daughter, Chantal. Chantal had returned to the states a couple of times after her year with the family back in 1975. Under the rules of the American Foreign Student exchange program, she had to wait two years before returning to the United States. She came back in August of 1977 and spent a month with the summer company on board the Whippoorwill. Then, she returned again during the summer of 1981, shortly after her marriage to André Gilbert. By Christmas of 1983, they had a darling and delightful 18-month old son, Raphael, who was walking and beginning to talk.

The couple made their way to London right after Thanksgiving and spent two weeks with Maggie. They saw many museums, churches, the Tower and a show virtually every night. They became quite adept at getting around via the underground transportation and found everyone to be so helpful when they would lose their way. In mid-December they crossed the channel to make their journey to Paris where they spent a few days with Chantal and André before beginning their tour of Germany. Crossing the channel was an experience in itself. They had to go by ferry, because the water is so unpredictably rough during the winter months that the hovercraft is not always running. The trip by ferry is normally six hours or so. First, however, they had to take the train from London to Dover where they would catch the ferry. The white cliffs of Dover—Veda thought that was just a figure of speech, but she found that they really are as white as the song implies. The sea was rough that day for the ferry crossing and many passengers were either sick or queasy looking. Bruce and Veda apparently had their sea legs, as the trip didn't make them sick, just tired from the length of it. Once the boat had reached Calais, they had another train ride into Paris, where they were met by André.

Chantal and André were at this time living in a very nice two-bedroom apartment above a bakery in the Paris suburb Bougival. Being the winter season, there were no flowers, but the leaves were still on many of the trees and the whole area around Paris seemed like a fairy tale to the couple. Chantal and André took the couple on a brief motor tour of the capital, pointing out various landmarks. One Saturday, they also drove to Chartes where they saw the famed cathedral with its beautiful stained glass windows, and they continued on to Versailles to tour King Louis' palace and grounds.

After spending a few days with their young French family, the couple boarded a train for Germany. They traveled through Belgium and stopped in the city of Aachen, which is very near the Netherlands border. Veda's brother, Bill, who was killed in action March 31, 1945 just a few weeks before VE Day, is buried in a military cemetery near Herleen, Netherlands. From Aachen, they boarded a bus to take the day trip to the Margraten-Netherlands American Cemetery. They found the caretakers at the cemetery very pleasant. Eager to show the couple around, although they have thousands of visitors every year, they don't often have immediate family members stop in. And, that very cold, damp December day, there were no other visitors. They were treated royally by the cemetery staff, who took them out into the cemetery to find Bill's grave.

From Aachen, they made their way to Hamburg, where they took a smaller train north to the small city of Heide which is near the North Sea close to Denmark. Bruce's maternal great-grandmother, Anna, had left Heide to emigrate to the U.S. when she was twenty-four years old. They found the city hall and enlisted some help to find his heritage in the town's records. They found the birth of his great-grandmother, her two sisters and then, the death (by hanging) of his great-great grandfather. Why? The man had been a *hufschmidt* (blacksmith) and the record gave no reason for the hanging. It was a few years after that event in 1855 that his great grandmother arrived in Chicago where she later met his great-grandfather and they came to settle in western Kansas.

While in London, the two had taken a weekend to drive with Maggie up to the city of Norwich (which is also on the coast of the North Sea on the east shore of England) and were able to trace Veda's maternal grandfather's roots. She found the record of her great-great grandparents' marriage. She was awed by that. So, the trip to Heide had been, in a way, a means to help piece together the mid-19th century map of the city of her birth that Bruce's great grandmother, and later his grandmother, had saved for years and which was now in tatters. Still legible, it was very faded and frayed.

Their trip also took them to Cologne, where Veda asked in her fractured Deutsch, "Wo ist der Dom?" The stationmaster at the train station responded, "Der Dom?" And she said, "Ya, wo ist der Dom?" He looked at her with a smirk of disgust and pointed, "Right there!"

She and Bruce laughed so hard over that incident. (Surely the stationmaster did, too.) She had been watching through the windows of the train for several minutes before they reached the city, because she had read in her college German studies that the noted cathedral was visible for miles around. She was thus disappointed that she had not been able to see it. Well, no wonder! The station was located right next to the cathedral and it was so large, one had to walk across the street in order to see the structure. Talk about awe!

From Cologne they went south with no idea of where they would get off the train. Remember, this was a time before the breakup of the USSR, so the train took them very close to the East German border. Bruce dozed a good portion of the trip, but Veda sat in their compartment, with eyes totally fixed on the scenery. She didn't want to miss a thing. Sure enough, as the train rounded a bend, a castle came into view. She'd read about castles that dotted the landscape of Germany and France; this is what she came to see. As they neared the city of Wurzburg, they decided to get off at that stop.

Wurzburg lies almost smack dab in the middle of Germany. It was one of the cities that suffered severe bombing during WWII. In 1983, almost forty years after the fact, there were still stark signs of destruction. One of the many churches the couple visited shocked the couple with the damage that it had sustained. The parish had evidently decided to leave the damage, or preserve it, actually, as a monument to World War II.

Everywhere the couple traveled, they tried to find some theater to attend. So, they perused the daily paper in Wurzburg to see what was playing. "*Nicht Gut, Nicht Schlect*," Bruce stated. "Something by C.P. Taylor, whoever that is."

"Not good, not bad," Veda mused. "Bruce, C.P. Taylor! That must be *Good*. Remember? That was one of the plays we saw on Broadway and were so stunned by it!" She was excited that it must be the same play about how a "good" man becomes swept up in the wave of the Nazi movement, to the point of rejecting his wife, his best friend (a Jew) and even his own mother. Everything happens so gradually, and the actor dances around to the music that a small ensemble provides as part of the action, until finally the man is caught up in the movement and becomes, himself, a Nazi. Deeply moving, they were anxious to see how well they might understand the play in the middle of Germany in the German language.

The theater audience was filled with older citizens (they are, after all, the society who can afford to attend the theater, right?). Older, rather, they were certainly old enough to have been very possibly involved in the movement of the 30's and 40's. Veda and Bruce whispered that they must not speak—they didn't wish to be known as American—not in the middle of an audience with wartime memories quite different from theirs. In fact, it was a puzzle as to why the play had been scheduled at this theater? Maybe, there was a shame here—or maybe, the members of this theater had been on the side of the allies. Or, well, they could muse for hours but they decided to just sit back and enjoy the show.

Their worries were really for naught. Although they perceived the audience "watching" them, and perhaps they were, no one spoke to them. And, they all seemed very nice. The play was well done, or so they thought in their limited understanding of the German language, and the evening was actually one of the most memorable theater experiences they ever had.

The next evening after Wurzburg, they were scheduled to be in Zurich to visit a friend who had spent several weeks at the playhouse in 1982. Susanna Suter. Susanna had come to Vassar with her sister who was living near Topeka to eat on the train and see a show. She enjoyed the ambiance of the place and asked to stay for a few days. She ended up staying a month through the end of that season working to help the couple on the train or assisting in the daily work of the players. Trained in homeopathic healing and massage, everyone came to rely on the soothing hands of Susanna. She would put her hands on the aching flesh ever so gently and begin to work lightly and slowly. The rhythm of her hands along with the gentle massage created a healing sensation for tired overworked muscles.

Susanna greeted the couple at the Zurich train station and insisted that they stay with her while there. They were to meet her parents who graciously invited them to have supper in their apartments one evening, and Susanna gave her American guests an extensive tour of the city.

From Zurich they continued by train into Austria to Innsbruck and, again, were struck by the beautiful scenery through the Alps. There was lots of snow, of course, and the old thatched roofed homes (cottages) caught their eyes. Along the journey there was one point at which the train rounded the bend of the mountain and, lo, a castle was located practically right on the train tracks sitting high among the evergreens in the mountains. What an incredible sight.

From Innsbruck, they continued on an overnight trip to Milan, Italy. On the trip through the mountains (by night this time) they were joined in their compartment by two young men, one of whom was from America, the other from France. They were male models for an international magazine. They lived in Milan and began telling the couple of all the sights they <u>must</u> see while in town and the food they must sample. When they arrived very early in the morning, both were quite fatigued from the journey and set about looking for a hotel. Usually, upon entering a strange city, they would first visit the American visitors' center that was normally located in the train station. In Milan's station, however, the American visitors' center had been bombed the day before, so it was not available, and their fractured Italian was even more meager than their use of the German language. A gentleman on the train had insisted they stay at the American Hotel, so, not knowing any other hotel, they set about finding it.

It is here that one should discuss the means of inner city travel in Europe. The cities all have good public transportation in their subway systems. By the time the couple had reached Milan (10 or 12 days into the 2-week journey) they had become quite adept at reading a map to find where their destination was located and the right train to get them to that stop. Also, everywhere along the way they had found many English-speaking individuals. They could stop almost anyone on the street, ask something in English and get an appropriate and helpful response. In Milan, however, it was different. After they had found their hotel, registered, had breakfast, and got a little rest, Bruce decided to make his way to the La Scala Opera House. Veda had requested that with their trip to Europe she wanted to see an opera at La Scala. And they were here!

"I walked to the subway stop and there was no one around. It was around 8:30 a.m. I waited for quite awhile. Two or three people came to wait, but otherwise, there was no one there. Pretty soon, I could hear a train coming and presto! The station was immediately filled. Totally! When the doors of the train opened, thousands got off and millions got on. I was shoved, pushed, stepped on and sworn at. At least, by the look on their faces I'm certain they were shouting swear words." He related to Veda the perils of his trip to the square and La Scala.

"You must come with me. There is a museum at La Scala. And we can go to the box office to try for same day tickets after 10:00 a.m." So, Veda, who had not felt well once they hit the Italian border, got out of her sick bed and made the trip back to the square with Bruce. They also determined to return by noon to vacate their room at the very expensive hotel and try to find a more reasonable pensione. Their luck with such housing had proven to be worth the less luxury for the benefit of having more money to spend elsewhere. They had budgeted just so much per day and they found that they were at the time well within their budget.

The opera for that evening was Puccini's *Turendot*. Singing the lead tenor was Placido Domingo. They were able to obtain tickets and they walked up and around and further up until they found themselves at the top of the house. Back row top balcony. What a view! Center stage. The orchestra began, the curtain opened and both of them sat motionless through Act I. When the act curtain descended, Bruce asked, "Well, what do you think?"

"I feel I have died and gone to heaven!"

Bruce felt the same way. It was a total phenomenon for them. It was grand opera that they had never before experienced. The stage that they had been privileged to see during their tour of the theater's museum and house tour earlier in the day was transformed by magic into a fantastic set. The couple agreed that the singers were just as magnificent.

"Thank you, God, for letting me have this once-in-a-lifetime experience!" Veda clasped her hands in gratitude.

After two days in Milan, they made reservations to take the RTV from Marseilles to Paris on December 23rd, so they would be able to be back at Chantal's in time for Maggie's birthday on Christmas Eve. She was to come from London and all of them spend Christmas together. So, the couple had to leave Milan to go along the coast of the Mediterranean toward Marseilles. Their train was to leave Marseilles around noon on the

23rd and it was now December 21st. The station in Milan was packed. It seemed everyone had somewhere to go just before Christmas. By the time their train backed into the station, there were thousands waiting for what appeared to be their train! Veda stood on the edge of the platform almost fearful that someone would push her over onto the tracks. Thankfully, nobody did, and the train stopped with the door for first class exactly at her spot. She easily stepped onto the train. Poor Bruce, however, was stuck several persons back with the luggage.

"You find a compartment and come back to let me push the suitcase through the window."

She did find a compartment and threw her coat across one of the seats and threatened the fellow passenger to save her seat. Then, she ran back to the hallway and found Bruce still on the platform pushing the suitcase through the open window. She pulled it onto the train as throngs of persons continued to board. As she watched her usually well-mannered husband, he pushed aside a lady and jumped aboard the train as it was beginning to move out of the station.

"Where are all of these people going, for heavens sake?"

There were people in the halls, in the compartments, out on the platforms between cars, everywhere! Most of them did not have first class tickets, so they were taking up space where they were not supposed to be. But, the train was packed. Where else could they go? The couple noticed that the conductor just sort of ignored what class tickets the passengers had as he came through checking.

They sat back and tried to enjoy the scenery as the train rolled along the tracks westward into southern France. They passed Monaco and marveled at how the mountains appeared to stretch their legs down to the sea. It was so beautiful that when the train pulled into Nice, the couple decided to just get off and see that city. They wouldn't have much time as they would need to continue on to Marseilles the next morning fairly early, but they could at least spend the evening in Nice. Everything's nicer in Nice.

Nicer? Well, the weather was cool, no, it was cold, especially for southern France. They walked out to the beach, but it was just too chilly to really enjoy it. So, they went to a cafe near the hotel they had found and had a fish dinner for two that was probably the most fish they had ever seen on one plate. Petites poissons, they were tiny and delectable.

The next morning they again boarded the train to make their connecting reservation on the RTV and continue toward Paris. The train trip from Marseilles to Paris took them through wine country and again, they saw castles in the hills. They had often heard Chantal rave over the beauty of the "South of France" and they had finally come to realize the truth she spoke.

* * *

On Christmas Eve, Maggie's golden birthday—she was twenty-four on the 24th—they walked through the wooded Bougival to attend a Christmas Eve service at a local Catholic church. Bruce and Veda were amazed to find the service to be similar to the church of their own childhood, the Quenemo Federated Church. It was very informal, there were lots of families in attendance, and the music was really terrible. There was congregational singing and "Père Noel" (Santa Claus) came—it was just like home, they thought!

Christmas in Bougival. Bruce, André, Chantal and Maggie 1983.

Christmas Day brought presents for everyone and Chantal served a feast with many courses. It took several hours to complete her sumptuous meal. She and André had purchased their apartment located over a wonderful bakery. Veda and Bruce would awaken each morning to the fragrance of bread baking in the large ovens outside. André would run down to pick up "baguettes" and fresh French butter. That was a feast in itself, but Chantal served much more on Christmas Day. There was a soup course, then meat, then vegetables, followed by a salad. Throughout, André had selected appropriate wines to complement the fine food. Chantal had also prepared a delectable dessert and, finally, a course of chocolates. Les Pyreneens. A French chocolate that is available only in France only during the Christmas holidays. Veda and Bruce were able to smuggle a few boxes of the sweets back to Kansas.

Maggie returned to London shortly after Christmas Day, but Bruce and Veda stayed with their young friends through New Years. They visited the Louvre, the Notre Dame, the Sacre Coeur Cathedral, and the Cimetière du Père Lachaise, where they took rubbings of the gravestones of Sarah Bernhardt, Gertrude Stein, Oscar Wilde, Frederick Chopin, and others. When questioned by André, "Why on earth did you go there?" it was hard for them to explain what a high it was for them to walk among the graves of so many artists. And, it was free!

They also visited Maxim's which was definitely <u>not</u> free. As they were making their way to Notre Dame, they had passed by the little cafe and Veda noted, "Bruce, here is Maxim's! Let's go in for lunch." So, they walked in, into the legendary cafe. They were stopped at the door with a gesture that seemed to suggest (or demand) they check their coats. Well, they had been traveling for three weeks and the weather bounced back and forth between rainy and snowy, so there was always mud. And most of it seemed to cling to Veda's one good cloth coat. She took off her coat and gave it to the gentleman all the while noting the furs and beautiful wraps hanging in the cloakroom. Ah well, another reason for hating the ugly "cheap" (and dirty) American!

The couple was escorted to a table where they could view the beautiful stained glass skylight and the gorgeous mirrors on all of the walls. An intimate cafe, it was beautifully decorated. They were given the menu, which they read long enough to realize that even with their newly found oil money, Maxim's was way out of their league. They ordered. Veda requested a salad. Bruce ordered a loaf of bread and a glass of water. They both asked for a glass of wine. The salad and the bread they shared and it was enough for their lunch. They figured up the bill in American dollars after they had left the cafe. "Sixty-four dollars, Bruce. That lunch cost us $64.00!" Not in their budget. What was André going to say about their having lunch at Maxim's?

"Oooh la la! That is so expensive. Don't ever go there again." André chided his friends. Bruce and Veda never told him the cost of their lunch. But that experience gave them something to remember and laugh about for years to come.

The couple journeyed back to London to spend one more week with Maggie before returning home. They had seen many plays on the trip, but Maggie said she would get tickets to Placido Domingo's conducting debut of *Die Fledermaus* at the Covent Gardens Opera. Having just seen him in *Turendot*, they felt it appropriate to see if he could conduct, too. He could. That performance was also televised and they were to see it on public television for years thereafter always saying, "We were sitting about there." And they would point somewhere in the direction of the balcony stage left.

Chapter Twenty-Four

While they were away on their European trip, the couple had arranged for Marla Wiens to live in their mobile home and take care of the mail during their absence. They had already set the summer season and had sent out the Christmas season ticket mailing just before leaving for London. Marla handled all of the subscriptions and kept track of the deposits. The couple had also arranged for her to be a temporary signer on their accounts for the month of December, so she was able to keep bills current, as well. The company had been released late October, and only Marla had stayed behind. The train, which was open during the fall for brunch on Sundays was closed for the winter, but every day someone would have to check things. The water was off on the train except for the kitchen car. It had to be checked daily to ensure the heat had not failed and that the water lines hadn't frozen. If they thought the summers at Vassar were frantic, the winters were a nightmare. Always problems somewhere.

For Marla, the problem was in the bunkhouse. Years earlier the couple had dug a pit on the south end of the bunkhouse and installed a greenhouse. Well, it was supposed to be a greenhouse; Bruce had planned it to have a gravel pit and concrete walls. He built the forms for the walls making sure they were level and as high as he needed; then he called for the cement to be delivered. The truck came and began pouring at which time the forms began to break. "Stop!" he hollered, "Stop pouring!" The truck driver explained that he had to pour ALL of the cement. "Do you want me to pour it on the parking lot?" "No, we'll just have a cement floor!" By the time the truck was empty, the cement floor was 3-4 feet thick! Thereafter, they referred to the greenhouse as "Bruce's launching pad!"

Veda's plants! The bunkhouse was heated by a wood burning heating stove. Although the bunkhouse was fairly well insulated, it wasn't totally impervious to the elements. Someone needed to build a fire and "stoke" it during the cold weather. Well, one night during the 1983-84 period, a cold spell hit with the temperature dropping below zero in just a few hours. Marla was gone at the time (it was fairly mild when she left) and when she returned, the bunkhouse plants had frozen. She felt very bad about it, but by the time the couple had returned Veda had forgotten what plants she had lost!

The company would not resume until summer. The couple said goodbye to their *other* daughter, Marla, and she moved to Kansas City to find work.

* * *

Veda had been planning to purchase a computer. She had been reading about them and her friend, Carole Lynes, had often said, "The playhouse would benefit from a little Apple. Word processing becomes so easy." Veda had the month of February 1984 available to learn, so she went shopping for a computer at the end of January and purchased an Epson QX-10. The salesman at the shop delivered it to the playhouse and set it up for her on a card table in the living room of their mobile home. He gave her a quick 15-minute lesson and suggested she come into the shop (Topeka) to take some classes.

"I don't have time to go to classes," she responded, "I have just this month of February and must be able to get the mailing list set up and be able to send a mass mailing and get the books set up on the accounting software by the first of March."

She then spent the next month glued to her new screen, reading instructions, taking the lessons that came with the computer, all the while reveling in her new toy.

"Don't you think you should come to bed? It's after 3:00 a.m.?" Bruce would find her sitting at the computer day and night. But, by March 1st she announced,

"Okay, I've learned how to use the computer. I can do a mail merge. I have the books setup, I can create graphs with the spreadsheet program. I can do it." The young salesman drove out to Vassar to follow-up his sale, a six-week checkup so to speak, and he pronounced her the "quickest student I have ever seen."

"Determined, that is what I was! Deadlines will do wonders for progress."

The following summer 1984 opened with *Hello, Dolly* with Bruce and Veda in the roles of Horace and Dolly. Rick was hired to direct the season. The directors of the KRFA (Kathryn Rogers Foundation for Artists) made the decision to manage the summer season at the barn. So, Lakeside Players would manage the food side of the summer, offering meals on the train, and KRFA the artistic side, producing plays in the barn. Also, KRFA was still looking for some way to keep a company year round and Bruce was that spring in process of negotiating for a space in Kansas City. By May he had almost decided on working with the people at the Folly Theater and he had invited the management to come to Vassar to see the opening show. Apparently, they enjoyed the evening and the couple thought a partnership was in the making. They were so sure they had a deal that they had included a blurb about wintering at the Folly in their season program. Several weeks into the summer, however, when the Folly brought out their contract and Bruce was ready to sign on behalf of the Foundation, he noted the theater had practically doubled the rent they had first quoted. No deal! And he came back to Vassar disheartened and disgruntled, but ready to continue looking for a space.

* * *

Chris returned home from the Navy that summer and Maggie, too, left London to return to the states. Other players returning that season were Margret Fenske, Lauri Boyd and Glynis Jones, who was to serve all summer in an apprentice position. New faces included Scott Cordes, Deidre Dorscher, Del Rinehart, Pam Anson, Doug Henry, Raymond Peat, Lynnae Lehfeldt, Matt Robinson and David Young, who came to Bruce and Veda before the season began to announce that he and Maggie had decided that whatever they did they were going to be together. During the three-year period she was in London, he had spent one year with her, then, when his visa expired, he had come home. After several months, he tried to return to London—arrived at the airport and, while going through Customs, he was questioned. They found that his Visa was not good and they put him right back on the plane to return to the U.S. He was barred from the British soil! By May he wanted to join Maggie again, and he let the couple know he was available for the summer, too. Bruce and Veda had admired the young man's work as an actor many times and were eager for him to join the company. Maggie did not arrive until the day before the opening of *Dolly*. On the heels of *Dolly* came *Annie, Funny Girl,* and finally, the musical revue of Cole Porter's music, *Cole*. All of the musicals were designed and built with the idea of moving to Kansas City.

The opening tableau for *Hello, Dolly!* 1984.

Bruce made many trips to KC looking at various spaces. He considered the Uptown Theater at Broadway and Valentine; he also considered an abandoned Firestone store. He even considered a vacant restaurant space in Olathe. Finally, sometime toward the end of July he came home from a Kansas City trip and told Veda,

"I've just come from a meeting with Judge Turpin." (Judge Turpin was the name of the evil judge in *Sweeney Todd*.)

"Who?" she asked.

"Well, his nails are polished and his hair is groomed meticulously, and he is a Jackson County judge that positively oozes with corruption."

He had come from looking at a building located at Armour Boulevard and Main Street that had formerly been a nightclub. "The space is great. It has a good location and would make a great theater. I just don't know whether or not I can stand to work with that man." He was talking about his next landlord.

Chapter Twenty-Five

The company thought the building at 19 East Armour Boulevard was going to be perfect for their urban theater. It had a parking lot that seemed sufficient for their audiences. The theater was formerly a night club and the stage area had been the section that housed the dance band, with an oak parquet dance floor in front of the "stage." The audience sat at tables, and the house held approximately 200 persons. Just right. They were used to a small stage, it could work. They would not try to play as a proscenium stage, but more as a thrust, creating their sets to come on down into the dance floor portion. It would make a perfect stage.

The judge had insisted on a letter of credit from Bruce. It was arranged and he and Veda met with the judge to go over the inventory of tables, chairs and equipment in the building and to sign the lease agreement which was between Judge Romano and his wife and the Kathryn Rogers Foundation For Artists. The inventory included such items as bar guns, which the paper said were working, tables, chairs and office furniture and other furniture in the basement, which was very musty and mildewed. Nothing was noted on the inventory of the mildew in the carpets and on the basement walls. There was a strong smell, but the couple felt that with some dedicated time for cleaning and several days of airing with the fans blowing, the basement could be made into a rehearsal space, shop and office area. They were determined. The name of *Theatreworks* went up on the marquee outside.

The couple hoped to be able to get a liquor license at some time in the future. The plays had first priority, however, so they negotiated with a nearby cafe to cater food and drink for the patrons. They didn't intend to serve dinners, just some light food, and the cafe had a license to serve liquor.

The opening show was *Hello Dolly*, with Bruce and Veda recreating their roles of Horace and Dolly. The music had been pre-recorded for the Vassar production and the company had closed their summer season with a one-week reprise of the show, so, other than adapting the set to fit the new space, that show was virtually ready to open. Some new chorus persons were added and David Young, as director of the KC production, changed some of the blocking to bring the action on down to the audience. It didn't take many rehearsals before the show was ready to go.

Earlier in the summer Rick had planned to continue with the Kansas City company, but his plans changed. He had completed his graduate degree at the University of South Carolina, and during the spring had interviewed for some positions. In July a job opened and he left Vassar early August, taking Big Kitty with him this time. He moved to Raleigh, North Carolina to teach theater at Peace College.

In the meantime, Maggie was handling the publicity. She put a blitz of radio and newspaper advertisements into the metropolitan area. Kansas City soon realized the *new kids* were in town. She also developed a mailing list and sent out a brochure offering season tickets prior to the company moving into KC. Results were beginning to come in. The pre-season sales were not very strong, but they were "hopeful."

Opening night arrived with a respectable house, albeit mostly complimentary seats they had offered the press and other theater personages in town. The house was chiefly non-paying customers, but they felt that word of mouth publicity was the best, so "give them a good show."

David had blocked Dolly's opening entrance on a bicycle and one evening, as she came wheeling to the stage, Veda's skirt got caught in the spokes of the back wheel. She was flying in as usual, delivering her first line to Ambrose Kemper (played by David) from the bicycle. She continued as blocked into the wings (with the sound of a "Crash") where she was to jump off the two-wheeler and come back onto the stage. As it happened that time, she was caught and couldn't get away from the contraption. She continued extemporaneous dialogue from the wings (while the action onstage remained frozen), hoping someone would come to extract her from the bicycle. Ultimately, Kathy Stengel, the stage manager, came to her rescue and Mrs. Levi finally made her way to the stage, bedraggled and looking frazzled as if she had come out of a wreck. (Which, indeed, she had!!) But, the skirt wasn't torn!

Dolly was scheduled to run three weeks and it was a disappointing run because of the small houses. The press didn't come—at least, not the reviewer from the Kansas City Star, and that was the biggest disappointment. The company was determined to hang in there, so they forged ahead with rehearsals for their second show, *HMS Pinafore*, holding open auditions for some of the roles and this brought some new faces to their stage.

The orchestra was live for *Pinafore*: Veda on piano accompanied by a violin, viola and cello—a piano quartet. The musicians worked from a piano score, figuring who should take which line and where to ensemble, etc. It turned out to be a delightful orchestra and didn't overpower the singers at all.

Following *Pinafore* was *Cole,* the revue of Cole Porter songs which had also played at Vassar during the previous summer season and which still maintained the same Vassar cast of players. It was a one-set show and had been designed to move to the Kansas City stage, so it required little rehearsal. More importantly, by this time at least, very little money was needed to prepare for production. Audiences continued to be low even though the company passed complimentary tickets to persons they felt might help push the new playhouse in town. The shows were well rehearsed and fast paced. They wouldn't apologize for the product, it was good. But the patrons didn't come. Only one evening, during the run of *Cole,* did they have even close to a full house. That was because of a large group that included Theatreworks into their convention planning. (Probably due to the fact that the wife of one of the organizers was Bruce's cousin!) Veda became more and more worried about the mounting accounts payable.

After *Cole* closed, the company mounted a production of *Annie* with the principals from the summer production, as well as some of the children. Other children from the Kansas City area were added to the cast. The production had been a sellout almost every night during the four-week summer run. In fact, all of the 1984 summer season sold quite well and the season at Vassar had ended with all bills paid and some money left over to go into the Kansas City venture. It wasn't enough! By December, when *Annie* was opening, Veda had to ask that the actors hold their paychecks. It was embarrassing. She was then able to borrow enough money to pay the salaries and some bills, but most were becoming very past due and she didn't know what she was going to do. They had begun receiving moneys for season ticket sales for the next summer at Vassar, but those sales, too, were down considerably from the previous year. It was going to be a bleak Christmas. She felt like she was constantly harping about the lack of money which seemed to create a pall around her; she was unable to enjoy the people working with her, nor the delightful productions they were able to scratch together. She and Bruce had always worked on a shoestring—but this venture was just too much for them. The rent alone was $4,500 each month. She didn't know whether that was comparable to other spaces of the same size or not, but she knew it was too expensive for them. So, Bruce tried to think of alternate uses for the building on the theater's dark nights.

He found that he could rent out the building for private parties and he discovered somewhat of a demand for that service. The only hitch was it didn't meet with the approval of a proactive homeowner down the street and, being the neighborhood activist that she was, she made several complaints regarding the noise or the patrons in the parking lot or anything else she could dredge for complaint. She had lived in her beautiful home at the time the building was a night club, and she wanted to ensure that it did not repeat the trouble in its checkered past. Evidently its closure was due to an outburst one evening that resulted in a shooting. That incident occurred several years earlier, but no matter how much Bruce or Veda tried to reason with the woman, she wasn't about to believe *they* were honorable persons. The mere fact that they *consorted* with the judge (Romano) was quite enough for her and she wasn't going to let them do anything, except legitimate theater. She never bothered them about the patrons attending the plays—just those who attended the parties. Did it have anything to do with the fact that most of the patrons attending the parties were black? And that the groups Bruce dealt with for the parties were generally minority groups? Who knows? As the revenues from the rentals grew, the couple found they had to cease pushing them, because the neighbor's clout also increased and she wasn't about to let there be any parties in that building. And that was that.

Before Christmas, the company set a new season for the spring, *Sweeney Todd*, *HMS Pinafore* (a reprise of the fall production), *Cloud Nine, Good* (the C.P Taylor play) and *Guys and Dolls*. New brochures were designed, printed, mailed and new expenses created. On New Years Eve, just before the opening of *Sweeney*, Veda drove to Lawrence to visit with Charley Oldfather about the not-for-profit theater's finances. She had worked with him during the winter of 1982, when he commuted from Lawrence to the Osage City Opera House to play in *Sleuth*. He had been so good in that production and the audiences, small though they were, loved him. When Veda had given him his contract check at the end of that run, he had refused it, and the action touched her. She knew he was a man of some wealth and she hoped he and his wife might be interested in helping KRFA.

She spent the afternoon visiting with Charley and his wife, Tensie, and it started to snow. It snowed so hard that by the time she left their country home south of Lawrence, there were eight or ten inches of accumulation on the ground and she worried that getting back to Kansas City might have its problems. With careful attention to driving, the little Mazda made it home.

"How did it go? Are they going to help?" Bruce was asking her the result of her meeting.

"Well, it's hard to say. They both are so nice and they were very receptive to our plight, but I don't know. I really don't. After all, why should they want to help our theater? Oh, by the way, I invited them to be our guest for *Sweeney*. They'll let us know when they want to come."

She truly didn't think they would call and was most surprised a few days later when Charley called to make reservations for the show. They came and apparently liked the production, especially, the talented players. But no mention was made of any monetary support.

With the monthly oil income Veda had managed to pay the rent and the salaries for January. As for the other bills, she kept putting the creditors off saying that she would soon catch up. The oil income had dwindled remarkably since the first checks and they were by then receiving only about $4,000 per month. The income would have been more than sufficient for the two of them, but not for a company of twelve. There was never enough.

On a Wednesday toward the end of January, Veda received a phone call and it was Charley. "Tensie and I were wondering if we could give you a little stock in the Burlington Northern Railroad. Her father gave it to her when she was just a girl. For us to sell it would mean a huge capital gains tax, so we thought we would just give it to you and you can do what you want with it."

"Oh, Charley, that is wonderful. You are indeed an answer to our prayers. I am stunned and very grateful. Thank you from the very depths of our hearts."

She then arranged to go to Lawrence to meet with the couple. Tensie would need to sign the certificate over to KRFA and have her signature guaranteed. The certificate was for 1,000 shares and the value at the time of transfer was around $55 per share. When Veda was saying goodbye and her thanks, Tensie also thanked her, "You have saved us quite a bit in capital gains tax." Veda couldn't believe it—she had no idea what capital gains taxes were.

Bruce and Veda felt the $55,000 gift was going to solve their problems. She paid the past due bills and there was still some money left over. They could hold their heads high.

In the meantime, Bruce had negotiated several parties for the theater's dark nights and he was trying to deal with those contracts and still keep a semblance of peace with their cantankerous neighbor to the south. Following *Sweeny Todd* was a three-week run of *Cloud Nine*. James Still (Jim Olson, aka Jim O from the summers of '76, '77, '78 and '79) had been hired to direct the show. After he had left Vassar and the University of Kansas, he moved to Chicago and found work as an actor. He had joined Actors Equity under the name of James Still, as there was already a James Olson. Among the shows he had played in Chicago, was a run of *Cloud Nine* at the Steppenwolf Theater. Bruce and Veda had also seen the Off Broadway production when they were in New York in 1982 and they were eager to have Jim come do the work. They were still very frugal on expenses, but they felt confident the season would pick up and they would get through the spring just fine.

The audiences for *Sweeney* had been very meager, and there was no review from the Star. They couldn't figure out what to do to get a review from the city's main newspaper. Veda had contacted that paper for years trying to get the reviewer to drive out to Vassar to see a show and always she got the same answer, "The Star does not do out of town reviews."

She knew that was false, for she had seen reviews of out of town shows. Nevertheless, that excuse didn't hold up anymore. They were in town now—right smack in the middle of mid-town, in fact. They deserved a review.

"The Star doesn't review community theater shows."

"This isn't a community theater! We pay our actors and technicians. There are some participants who are not paid, but the bulk of the company *is*."

The cast for *Sweeney* included the regular company members and was supplemented with some actors from the community. After Christmas several members of the company had left, including Pam Anson, Doug Henry, Lauri Boyd and Lynnae Lehfeldt. David Young, Scott Cordes, Glynis Jones and Raymond Peat stayed on, as well as the crew which included Chris, Kathy Stengel and Del Rinehart. Paul Soule came in to re-create his role of Toby in *Sweeney.* A friend of Jim Story's from UMKC joined the company to play Mrs. Lovett; Marla Wiens came in to sing in the chorus and Ray Peat played the title role. Brad Zimmerman who had been a part of the spring 1982 *"Grease* by correspondence" tour was cast in the role of Pirelli and another local actor was brought in to play Judge Turpin. Bruce directed the show and Margret Fenske drove up each evening from Osage City (approximately 150 miles round trip) to be the "orchestra." Maggie had gone before *Sweeney's* end when she had accepted a position as publicist for the Old Creamery Theater in Garrison, Iowa. The couple then brought in Gail Bronfman to help with managing the box office and publicity. After *Sweeney,* Ray Peat also left the company.

Once James arrived in town for *Cloud Nine* rehearsals, he contacted the Kansas City Star, himself, and whatever he said must have worked. Robert Butler, who was the Star's theater critic at the time, came to Theatreworks to interview James. What's more, he came back and reviewed *Cloud Nine.* A rave review! And the houses picked up. The cast for the show included some of James' old friends while at KU and who were now in the KC area: Kathleen Warfel, Mark Rector (he'd been in *Working* during 1983), Julie Broski and Lisa Heffley. Company members included David Young and Scott Cordes. By the final performance, they knew they had a hit. It was hard for them to close it and go on to the next show, but they stuck to the schedule which included a one-week run of *HMS Pinafore,* followed by C.P. Taylor's *Good.* Butler came back to review *Good.* Not a rave review, but favorable. David Young played the "good" German who dances his way around life into Nazism. His Jewish friend, Max, was played by David Herrin. Veda played the man's senile mother about whom he rationalizes the benefits of genocide. Ron Freeby, who was by then a member of the Foundation's board of directors, came in to help with the show by playing the Hitler character. Marla, who was also living and working in KC, joined the company to play the wife (ex-wife). Artistically, it was a good show, but the audiences dwindled. Whether it was the topic or what, no one could explain the fickleness of theater audiences.

By the time *Guys and Dolls,* their final show of the Kansas City season, had opened, they had used up the windfall from the Oldfathers and were back in the hole. Bill Christie was then president of the KRFA board and he agreed to direct the musical. He hired Jeanne Beechwood to do choreography. For their final show of the spring season, the cast was comprised almost entirely of community actors. The crew remained, but of the original company members, there were just Scott Cordes and Glynis Jones left. The set was designed by Rick Rottschaefer, the concept being that it could then move to Vassar to open the 1985 summer season.

* * *

Bruce and Veda had decided to open the train at Vassar on Easter for brunch, then, Sundays only until June, when they would open for the summer season. On the Saturday before Easter, they drove to Vassar, stopping in Ottawa to shop for the supplies that they would need for the next day's brunch. On the way down to Ottawa, they were not very cheerful.

"This is really ridiculous—stopping at a grocery store to pick up supplies for brunch tomorrow. There is hardly enough money in the Lakeside Players account to pay the grocery bill and KRFA hasn't paid the rent for the use of the barn for last summer's season, nor does it look like funds will be there for this year. What in the world are we doing anyway?" Bruce was about ready to call it quits.

"What else can we do, Bruce? The SBA hasn't foreclosed. You've got a season set for the summer; some money has already come in and you've hired a cast. You can't afford to make refunds, so we have to go on. Might as well try to enjoy it!"

They did have the summer set and another great cast hired. They had contracted with Tom Mitchell to direct for the season and his wife, Joi Hoffsommer, agreed to appear in *The Miss Firecracker Contest*. The season would open with *Guys and Dolls*, then *Firecracker* followed by *Hans Christian Anderson* and ending with another musical, *Joseph and the Technicolor Dreamcoat*. Also returning to that Vassar season were Marla Wiens, Margret Fenske, Lynnae Lehfeldt and Bryan Jackson, who had worked on the train the previous summer. New faces were Robert Ball, Charles Bell, Mark Camacho, Greg Hunsaker, Joel Lillegraven, Lynne Rothrock, Greg Pospisil, Brian Sackett, Annamarie Pileggi and Joe Fox. Scott Moon served as Stage Manager and Julie Renner was Costumer for the season. As she stood in the wings awaiting her entrance as General Cartwright listening to Annamarie, in the role of Adelaide, sing "A person could develop a bad, bad cold!" from *Adelaide's Lament*, Veda remarked to Bruce, "She's good, really very good as Adelaide. So are the other actors. I'm proud to present this production." The Frank Loesser musical *Guys and Dolls* was probably their all time favorite. They loved the Damon Runyan stories and the characters adapted so honestly to the musical version. They especially loved the opening sequence where, in both of the Vassar productions, all of the characters eventually crossed the stage in a bit of business. The couple had been directly associated with six different productions and had seen the stage and/or movie version some six or seven more times.

"You can't go wrong with *Guys and Dolls*," they had always felt.

"So, why do we have half a house?" Neither of them could answer that.

Some years before they had added the train, they thought about air conditioning the barn. Now they wondered if it would have made a difference in the size of their houses. And yet, the summer of 1985 was starting out milder than many summers. Not even hot so far.

"In sixteen seasons, I have never been able to tell what draws a crowd. Look at how they flocked to *Annie* last year. And for the 1972 production of *Guys and Dolls*, we were sold out! It wasn't the weather that brought them or kept them away. The production this year is as good as 1972, so that's not it either."

They had always believed in motivation and work. Set your goal, work hard and you'll achieve success. It *should* happen. There wasn't a lot of competition. The nearest was Topeka's theaters, Washburn University and Topeka Civic Theater. True, they shared some audience members with Topeka, but competition was not a problem. One summer, near the close of the season, the couple had spent an off-Monday in Kansas City and, upon reading the theater section of the *Kansas City Star* to see what was playing, it was interesting to note the *only* listing was for (and this was in 1980) *A Little Night Music* at Vassar. No competition and audiences were still low.

Now, five years later, crowds were still low. "It will get better. Maybe the audiences are waiting for *Firecracker*." She was ever optimistic.

The Miss Firecracker Contest opened June 25th, just before the 4th of July, and played just two weeks with an average house of 95 persons.

"Less than half full!" she exclaimed. "What is wrong? The show is one of the better ones we have done."

Bruce agreed with her. By this time into the summer of 1985, he was so busy running back and forth between Vassar and Kansas City, trying to mollify the judge, their landlord, and keep him happy. They were almost two months behind in the rent for the Theatreworks building and Bruce had told her that one day when he was in KC, the judge had brought his attorney into the building and they spent their time examining the building and the properties, tables and chairs, etc., busily taking notes.

"What for? Is he going to find something wrong?" She asked.

"I hope not. Heaven knows the building is in fantastically better shape than when we went in last year." He said, "Nevertheless, I can tell he is looking for a way to collect on that letter of credit. We've got to get him paid."

"And the IRS, and the dairy bill, and the payroll, and the printer, and—" She let her voice trail. It seemed so futile. They worked hard; in fact, insofar as hired help, it was at a minimum both on the train and at the barn. Bruce had taken over most of the cooking in the kitchen. They had a helper, Genevieve Resor, whom they were able to depend on; but lacking the funds to pay more than a pittance, Bruce tried to do much of the prep as well as the evening shifts. Veda managed the front, greeting customers, overseeing the waiters and, many times, helping with the serving and bartending. Both of them took their turns at cleaning, too. And, they both looked in and conferred on the barn shows several hours daily. It wasn't as if they just sat back and let the money roll out the door. They were constantly involved in everything, trying to find the key to make it work.

They had mortgaged the farm near WaKeeney in the fall of 1980. When the oil money began coming in during 1982, they had planned to be able to pay off that debt quickly. But, they hadn't. The money was spent taking up the slack in each season's income statement. Now, the oil money had slacked off and a $45,000 debt on their property still remained.

"We'll figure out something, Bruce. We always do."

The next day the phone rang and Veda answered. It was a lady from the International Department at the First National Bank of Kansas City saying that Anthony Romano had presented her with a letter of credit, in the amount of $30,000 and that he intended to collect. Furthermore, the banker stated, she was unable to do anything except pay the credit, unless the couple were to get it legally stopped. Bruce was in Kansas City, somewhere, looking for a job; and she didn't even know where to contact him. She telephoned their attorney and talked to him—he asked her, "How much do you owe him?"

"I think it is a little over two months rent now—$10,000, I guess." She responded.

The attorney suggested she contact Bruce and wire $10,000 to their Kansas City bank for Bruce to collect and take a cashiers check to the judge. As luck would have it, Bruce telephoned her later in the day. She told him what had happened and the game plan. Then, she telephoned their local banker to see how they could raise the $10,000 to wire the judge. They had been lucky to have found a friend in their banker, Jon Wilhite. He laughed, "This judge sounds like a crook! What do you think?" She had no trouble telling him what she thought. "The problem is, Jon, that he would never do something illegal. Everything is perfectly legal. Morality does not enter the equation, but the law does. He will collect the entire $30,000, moral or not!"

"Well, $30,000 isn't a lot of money, but $10,000 is better. We'll get the funds to the judge this afternoon." It seemed like a lot of money to her.

Jon wired the $10,000 to their bank in Kansas City. Bruce picked up a cashier's check to take the judge. He wasn't available. So, Bruce contacted the judge's attorney and took it to him. The attorney signed a receipt for the funds, and Bruce went home thinking the problem was over. The next morning the same banker who had telephoned the day before, called again to let them know she had that morning paid the letter of credit. "How can you do that? We've paid our bill!" Veda was upset. The banker responded that everything appeared to be in order and that she had no choice but to pay it.

Bruce contacted the judge who told him he refused the check for $10,000, because, "you owe me $10,100!"

"So what are you going to do with the other $20,000?" Bruce asked him, "Will we get that back? And what about the $4,500 deposit we paid you last year?"

The judge explained that they would examine the building at the end of the contract and, if everything was in order, an adjustment would then be made.

Veda drove to meet with their banker that morning to explain what had happened and to figure out how they would meet the additional debt. She offered the mobile home where they lived and also, the house in Quenemo that they still owned, as collateral on their new loan. It was the last of any unencumbered property they owned.

Life still went on. They still had the season to finish—*Hans Christensen Andersen* and *Joseph and the Amazing Technicolor Dreamcoat*. They couldn't confide in anyone about their problems; because they felt by this time that all they did was cry for lack of money. It was an old song, and if it was so bad, how were they always able to go on? Well, they sat down together and decided that unless there were, by some chance, a real miracle, this would be the last time they would cry about lack of crowds, lack of money. They were through.

When the 1985 season at Vassar ended, they discussed the financial situation with their board of directors and decided to take the troupe to KC for a month of *Joseph* at Theatreworks. They reasoned that the rent was paid and they might as well use the space! Also, they had a few contracts to meet with regard to touring *Joseph*. As expected, the Kansas City production had some cast changes and some added rehearsals to accommodate the space. It turned out to be a very enjoyable production. Bruce and Veda were not terribly fond of Webber and Rice musicals; but *Joseph* had some freshness about it, as it was their first collaboration. They would watch the performance from the audience each evening with broad smiles, their money cares forgotten for a while.

The couple had rented an apartment near Theatreworks, where they lived when in Kansas City. It was small, although maybe not as small as the trailers they had been living in at Vassar since 1978. There was one large bedroom, a bathroom and a quasi-dressing room, a large living room, dining area and small kitchen that was overrun by cockroaches. It was their new home and it was in the middle of Kansas City, close to everything that was happening at the time.

After *Joseph* ended at Theatreworks in September, the players moved theater properties back to Vassar, cleaned everything thoroughly and locked up the train and the barn for the winter. Veda made arrangements for their final paychecks; then she and Bruce inspected the railroad car where their furniture had been stored for seven years, since October, 1978. They made the rounds of the other buildings: the rock house standing there since 1876, where the costumes were stored, the Regal Ruby, the sets and props cars and the bunkhouse/greenhouse(?). They even walked the grounds to look at the trees they had planted years before: the fruit trees, weeping willows, Russian sages, redbuds, two spruce trees, a smoke tree, and a cottonwood. Veda also checked the red rose briar in the front bed at the south edge of the parking lot, while Bruce took the footpath to the lagoon to look at the cattails. He had battled them every year, and still they persisted. He knew *they* would survive. After the final check of the 10-acre plot that had housed them, their children and their dreams for sixteen seasons, the couple locked up their mobile home. They had each other, had been married 29 years, were healthy, just 50 years old and still able to work. They took a last photo of their dream. They had dared to try.

Smiling at each other, they got into their seven-year old Mazda and turned on the radio: "Memories, light the corners of my mind—" Ah, Barbra! They drove home to Kansas City.

Vassar Playhouse 1985.

AFTERGLOW

In a story such as ours, the reader often wonders, "Well, what happened? Where are they now? Who is working in theater today? Where are the success stories?"

We have kept in touch these many years with lots of the young people who came through Vassar Playhouse, but not everyone. We've lost track of so many. Often when people ask me about our playhouse, they expect to hear that we produced a famous actor. Once in awhile someone will be looking at the photos on our walls and recognize Jim Reynolds as Abe Carver on *Days of our Lives*. As for fame, his face is probably the best known of all those who were at Vassar. But, we know that most of the players have gone on to make their mark on the lives of other young people, too, and yes, others have themselves found professional work in the theatre as actors, stage managers, costumers, directors, scenic designers, writers, producers, et al. It is gratifying to think Bruce and I may have had some measure of influence on those lives. Maybe. I don't know. I do know they certainly left an imprint on ours. So, here goes with what we know of some of our "kids":

1970

Ric Averill married **Jeanne Rice** (boy and girl in *The Fantasticks*); they moved to Lawrence and she taught high school speech and theatre while he founded and worked with his renowned children's theatre troupe, Seem to Be Players. The troupe has won national awards over the years; Ric and Jeanne have two children, the older of whom, Willy (named for Wilhelm von Vassar—the face on the barn) is a playwright, as is his father. Together they have several screen plays to their credit. Jeanne is an Equity actress in the Kansas City/Lawrence area.

Roger Cummings moved to Olympia, Washington, and worked for the state of Washington. Now retired, he continues to enjoy theatre productions, periodically working with various community groups. And he is still a talented, active artist.

Jane Stinnett became a pharmacist; she is married, lives in Lawrence, works in Topeka, but is active with the Lawrence Community Theater as actress and avid volunteer.

Marti Malik became an attorney, moved to Longmont, Colorado and married—we all know that attorneys love to act—he is surely no exception.

Stacy Scott lived in New York City and continued to pursue an acting career; having little luck she resumed work with an airline office. She contracted leukemia and died in Texas sometime during the 1980s.

Barbara Driver is now in a retirement home in Topeka (with my brother, Joe) and she continues to play piano weekly on Thursdays to entertain the other residents. She still knows all the old songs.

Dick and Ruth Driver still live in Topeka. Dick continued his education (Ph.D. from Kansas State University) while teaching and working as Math Supervisor in the Topeka School District's administrative offices. After he retired from that job, he was hired on to teach Math at Washburn University. Although he has announced retirement from there several times, he is still on the faculty, at least, part time. Ruth obtained her Masters degree in Art Therapy from Emporia State University and had a studio for years. She no longer teaches, but she still creates.

1971

Misty Maynard worked in Wichita as a teacher and established her own theatre, *The Kechi Playhouse*, in 1983. Still playing, you can check out her website at: www.kechiplayhouse.com/

Jim Reynolds moved to Los Angeles in 1974, and in 1981 he became Abe Carver on TVs *Days of our Lives*. He is easy to find on NBC as the longest-playing African American in a daytime television series. He was in the film, *Mr. Majestyk,* with Charles Bronson, and has played multiple television and film roles. He also organized and ran the Los Angeles Repertory Theatre for seven years.

Stuart Mossman (Mark Twain) founded the Mossman Guitar Factory in Winfield, building acoustic guitars for such stars as Glen Campbell,

David Carradine, Robert and Keith Carradine and others. He sold his business and went on to portray Mark Twain to schools and community groups. Stuart died of a massive heart attack in 1999.

John Friesen moved to Albuquerque and then, to Houston, where he worked in I.T. for various firms. He contracted the HIV virus and died in 1992. Always a lover of opera and musical theatre, his ashes were scattered over the grounds of the Santa Fe Opera.

1972

Martha Doty moved to Los Angeles where she found work with Walt Disney Productions. Ultimately she moved on to become a television producer working in New York, Chicago, and now in Houston.

Carolyn Harrison has continued performing and teaching voice. She lives in Denver; her two sons are now grown: **Joe** ("Auntie Mame's *little love*") lives in Cincinnati with his wife and two sons. He is a professional photographer. Ron lives in Minneapolis with his wife and two children.

1973

Rick Rottschaefer and **Sally Ann Wright**: well, we already know they married and then, divorced. Sally moved to Minneapolis, where she found work as an actress and then, married an actor and had two children. She is currently providing elder care for her aging parents who live with her. Rick moved to Raleigh, North Carolina, teaching at Peace College. He came out of the closet in 1985 and had a wonderful relationship with his partner, Jim. Rick died in January 1995, and Peace College has since honored his memory by establishing a scholarship and naming the green room at the college in his memory.

Bill Christie moved to Kansas City and became Equity Stage Manager for the American Heartland Theater. He is often called upon to direct plays for other professional theatres in and around Kansas City.

Mark Morehouse became a pastor and now lives in Beaver Dam, Wisconsin. (My experience has found that, like attorneys, ministers are practicing actors, too!)

1974

Vaughn Armstrong and **Chris Edsey** are married and have two sons. She and Vaughn live in Los Angeles. Vaughn has had a successful career in film and TV, appearing in the most roles in the *Star Trek* series from 1995 to 2005 (he is a favorite at the "Trekkies" conventions.) He has also appeared in many other films and television series.

Scott Lynes (*HMS Pinafore*, 1975 *Gypsy*, 1982-83) moved to Colorado and established a screen printing business in the living room of his apartment. Business grew and in 1987 he founded Imprints Wholesale, based in Denver. Today he has operations in four other cities: Seattle, Las Vegas, Kansas City, and Milwaukee. If you wear sports clothing at all, chances are good that it was distributed by one of his plants.

Stephanie Ratliff moved to the west coast where she lived several years and then, she returned to her home state of Kansas, married and with two children. Now divorced, Stephanie has obtained a teaching degree in Spanish and she is a teacher in the Kansas City area.

Phil Bachus lives in the Kansas City area, too, but I'm not sure what he does now.

Chantal Morin (our French daughter) lives in Le Mans, France with her husband, André. Their two children, Raphael and Mathilde, are both grown and both married in 2011. Mathilde will spend two months in Denver with Maggie and family during April and May 2012, while she serves an internship (at Imprints Wholesale, with **Scott Lynes**!) to satisfy her degree requirements. Sadly, her husband, Armand, is unable to join her. Raphael lives in Rio with his bride, Vivian. Bruce and Veda have visited Chantal in France several times. They were able to attend Mathilde's wedding last September, making the trip together with Maggie, John, Logan and Bolton.

1975

Lynn Gordon and **Will Hladik** married, moved to New York where Lynn worked as a casting director for the William Morris Agency. The couple divorced; Will moved to Omaha where he opened a music store; Lynn remarried, had a son and moved to Dallas. Divorced, she has done some casting in Dallas, but is now teaching theater and directing a youth theater group of the Dallas area.

Lisa Kessinger became a high school speech and debate coach. She is married and has two girls. She and her husband, Larry, live in Abilene and Lisa teaches at Dickinson Co High School in Chapman, KS.

Jan Feager remained in Kansas City a few years and then, she moved back to the St. Louis area of her youth. She performed with the Metro Theatre Circus for several years before marrying a stained glass artist, Tim Cosby. Jan is a dance teacher while home schooling their daughter, Etta, almost 17.

Jennifer Warner lives on Long Island and works for a catering company. She has a grown son, Cody.

Sara Driver became a professional violist and teacher. She now has her string studio in Austin, Texas, teaching and performing professionally in instrumental ensembles and recitals.

Greg Clevenger served in the US Marines Reserves after leaving active duty in Saudi Arabia as a helicopter pilot. He married and taught elementary school in the Phoenix area. He was killed in 2000 in a helicopter crash while on a USM Reserves training maneuver in Arizona.

Rick Brown worked as an actor in the Dallas/Ft. Worth area for years, but now lives in the city of his youth, Santa Rosa, California.

Deetra Driver lives in Topeka where she works as a coordinator for Washburn University and the Sunflower Music Festival.

1976

Tom Mitchell married **Joi Hoffsommer** (1977-1979); they have three sons, live in Champaign, Illinois, where Tom is on the theatre faculty of the University of Illinois/Champaign. Joi is a busy professional actress in the Champaign/Urbana area.

Larry Pressgrove worked with the St Louis Metro Theatre Circus for several years before moving to New York City. He is a conductor (*CATS* Broadway, touring productions for *CATS, Les Miserables, Phantom of the Opera* and others.) He has also served as conductor for many regional musical theatre productions; he was one of the collaborators and served as "orchestra" and Musical Director for the original *[title* *of show,]* and most recently their new production of *Now.Here.This.*, which opened at the Vineyard Theatre in March 2012.

Anne Abrams has worked as a publicist for many years, including the national tours for *River Dance*. She lives in California.

Scott Wible lives in the Minneapolis area where he works for McGraw-Hill publishers.

James Still (aka **Jim Olson**) first moved to Chicago and found work as an actor. Always a writer, he began an earnest career at playwriting in the mid-1980's and has since written many, many scripts, winning multiple honors and awards working in film, television and stage. He is Playwright in Residence for the Indiana Repertory Theatre, and most recently, he was elected to the National Theatre Conference and membership in the College of Fellows of American Theatre. A few of his plays include *The Heavens are Hung in Black* (commissioned for and premiered at the Ford's Theatre in Washington, DC 2009), *Iron Kisses, Looking Over the President's Shoulder, The Velvet Rut, And Then They Came for Me*, a film, *The Velocity of Gary, (not his real name),* starring Salma Hayek, Vincent D'Onofrio, Thomas Jane, and Ethan Hawk, directed by Dan Ireland. His television credits include the Discovery Kids series *Paz,* Maurice Sendak's *Little Bear* series, Bill Cosby's *Little Bill* series, and many more plays and awards too numerous to mention here. His plays are featured by Dramatic Publishing.

Nelson Warren: continued his teaching career, eventually working in the Andover, Kansas public schools teaching Speech and Debate garnering many honors for his debate teams over the years. He married **Beth Velasquez** (VP 1979). They have a daughter and have since divorced. Nelson has retired and still lives in Andover.

Aaron Gragg met his wife, **Marla Wiens** (1982-85), at Vassar. They married and have raised two children. Aaron works for Westar Energy in Topeka and Marla writes.

Debbie Kramer graduated from Emporia State University. She is married with three children and lives in Vassar, Kansas.

Wanda Wilhite (Whippoorwill 1976, *Sound of Music* 1979, Treasurer of KRFA 1980-1985) is retired from teaching. She and her husband, Jon still live in Overbrook.

1977

Diana Gish alternates working in radio and education. Today she is in Kodiak, Alaska with her three sons.

Karla Cherveny studied at Southwestern College, married and moved to Denver where she has worked in marketing and sales for many years. She has two sons (three, counting her step-son).

1978

Mark Swezey continued his teaching career: Tonganoxie (KS) High School, Shawnee Mission schools, Overland Park, KS and now is the Director of Theatre for the Jewish Community Center of Greater Kansas City.

Deborah Bremer worked a season for the Joseph Papp *Shakespeare in the Park*, before becoming a Methodist Minister. She now lives in Vermont.

David Ollington became a professional dancer and dance teacher and currently lives in Kansas City where he performs and teaches.

Susan Sublett is a teacher living in California.

Kevin Fewell works in Kansas City as an actor. We have seen him in some television commercials.

Julie Wilhite (*South Pacific*, 1978, *Sound of Music* 1979, *Miracle Worker* and *King and I* 1980, *Annie* 1984 and *Hans Christian Anderson* 1985) became a pediatrician and now practices in the Joplin, Missouri area.

1979

Jan Zabel became an opera singer and now lives and works in the Seattle area.

Keith Robison (from the train) became a journalist and now works for the Kansas City Star.

Barb Meier moved to Oregon where she married and raised three boys from her mountain home in Medford. She is now a fulltime elementary teacher.

1980

Dennis Lickteig moved to San Francisco. He is now Director of Operations for TicketWeb. He also serves as Director for many stage shows in the San Francisco/Oakland area.

Ron Freeby worked as properties master for Kansas City theatres for several years before he joined his partner in the antiques business. Now they own Mockingbird Antiques on Independence Square, Independence, Missouri.

Tim Counts moved to Minneapolis and found work with the federal government. He is also a contributing editor for *The American Bungalow* magazine. He said when he left Vassar, "I think I'll take a breather from theatre for awhile." And he did!

Andy Garrison founded his own Actor Training Studio in Kansas City, and continues to manage it while creating stage roles, voice-overs, and commercial work.

Lenette Steinle is a high school music teacher in the Kansas City area and works with the Gladstone Theatre in the Park.

Miles Norton lives in New York City; he works as a waiter while he continues to audition and act in periodic workshop productions.

Bill Ellwood became a banker; he lives in Overland Park, Kansas.

Wayne Cherveny worked for several years with the Kansas Turnpike Association. Now retired, he and his wife, Jane, still live in Winfield.

Roger and Allyson Moon moved back to Winfield, where they are co-directors of the Southwestern College Theatre Department.

Kristi Willhite continues to teach music and perform in the Lawrence area where she lives with her husband, Clint Liang. Her first husband, Mike, died of kidney cancer in 1987.

Carole Lynes (President of KRFA 1980-1983 and life-long friend/soul sister) lives in Arizona, while dividing her time between there and Minneapolis/Denver, where her two sons live. Her husband, John, died in 2000.

1981

Pam Kerrihard pursued an acting career for awhile, working on cruise ships. Ultimately she moved to Kansas City, where she is a homemaker, married with two children.

Karla Reisch lives in Manchester, Indiana. She is a writer.
Wendy Parman lives in Chicago where she has a voice and acting studio.

1982

Paul Soule moved to New York City and found work almost immediately as a dresser for *Les Miserables*, going on to work in costuming for other Broadway shows. He was Key Costumer for the movie, *Ride with the Devil*, directed by Ang Lee, and today he is Costume Supervisor for NBC's popular *30 Rock*.

Laure Ronnebaum went on to the University of Kansas to obtain a Masters in Vocal Performance. She has a voice studio in Olathe, KS and performs throughout the Metropolitan Kansas City area. She has three adopted children who otherwise give her something to do.

Lori Bryant has worked with not-for-profit theatre companies since leaving Vassar, but she now lives in Corpus Christi where she works for the Corpus Christi Museum of Science and History.

1983

LeWan Alexander attended Wayne State University and became a professional actor much in demand by regional theatres particularly for their Shakespeare productions. He died much too young. James Still helped to establish a scholarship in his memory at the University of Kansas. His legacy lives on.

Mark Rector worked for a time with Nebraska Theatre Caravan. He is now married, living in Chicago working for Lloyd's of London.

Margret Fenske has worked as costumer for the Cincinnati Playhouse and the Louisville Children's Theatre. She also sings with Sweet Adelines and continues to entertain with her piano skills.

Ron Meyer has been a high school theatre coach for years, working in the Kansas City Metropolitan area. He also often works for the University of Central Missouri, Warrensburg, coaching and directing in their summer theatre program.

Jim Story managed the Quality Hill Playhouse in Kansas City for several years before moving to New York City, where he now works and plays.

Gerry Prescott retired from teaching elementary school in the Ottawa Public Schools, moved to Colorado Springs where he embarked on a career in management of a medical clinic. He is finally retired now and still living in Colorado Springs.

Ellen Young continued to study ballet, ultimately opening her own dance studio in New York City. Following birth of her daughter, she moved out of the city and now teaches in upstate Dobbs Ferry, New York.

Howard Driver (Sweeney Todd at the Osage City Opera House) moved to Ottawa, where he worked for the Ottawa Truck. He married Jeanne in 2000. They live in Ottawa.

1984

Scott Cordes remained in Kansas City, finding work and becoming a professional actor in stage and film. Today he is certainly one of the busiest actors in town and considered to be one of Kansas City's most talented actors. His son, Sam, is also a well-known actor about town, as is his wife, Jen Mays.

Lynnae Lehfeldt studied at Wayne State University. She has done some acting and now is Assistant Professor of Theatre at Oakland University. She lives in Ann Arbor, Michigan with her husband and two children.

1985

Kathleen Warfel (Theatreworks *Cloud Nine*) has stayed in Kansas City where she works as a busy actress. She is also Director at Mid-American Nazarene University.

Joe Fox III remained in Kansas City where he is now Managing Director for the popular New Theatre Restaurant in Overland Park.

Kathy Stengel is still stage managing, currently working for the New Theatre Restaurant in Overland Park, a job she has held for many years.

* * *

The Rest of the Story

Eleanor Richardson moved her Winnebago permanently back to Winfield after her appearance in *Bus Stop* in 1980. She became the quintessential grandmother! Her daughters, **Ann** and **Beth** also live in Winfield. Beth has three kids and is a Methodist Minister and grandmother. Ann works as a bank compliance officer.

Maggie Rogers moved to Denver where she discovered the trade show exhibits industry. After working in the industry for several years, she and a partner founded Exhibit Logistics in 1999, and when the industry severely waned following the 9/11/2001 attacks, they had to close their doors in 2004. She went to work for Jeppesen in their corporate offices (Jeppesen is a subsidiary of Boeing) Tradeshows, Marketing and Communications department. She travels the world with Jeppesen tradeshow exhibits and says that managing a tradeshow is just like installing and striking a set! She has been married to John Hick since October 1995 and Veda's nine-year-old twin grandsons, Logan and Bolton, live with them.

Chris Rogers served almost ten years with the US Navy, working as Ship's Electrician. He left the Navy in 1992, and has worked at different electrical jobs since. He has recently completed a course in electrics graduating from Vatterott College, Kansas City, in June 2011, and today works in electrical maintenance for Kessinger Hunter in Kansas City, at the formerly Hyatt Crown Center.

Bruce Rogers worked two years as baker for an upscale restaurant, Café Allegro, in Kansas City while searching for a *real* job. In 1988 he went to work for the Kansas City Museum as Exhibits Manager, retiring in 2000. Today he reads, gardens and cooks breakfast for the couple's home-stay bed and breakfast, Gladstone Manor. Come visit www.gladstonemanor.com.

Veda Rogers worked at various temp jobs for a few months in 1985, before accepting a secretarial position in a Kansas City bank's loan department. Ultimately she worked for Central Bank of Kansas City as their Administrative Officer, the title being a cover for executive secretary, board secretary, compliance officer, and even I.T. officer. You can stop laughing now. She is retired and writing this book.

The SBA acquired the playhouse in 1986, and auctioned off the train cars, theatre props, costumes, and equipment, and then sold the real estate to a local couple who built a new home on the property and razed the 1876 rock house. About 1995 or so, another couple purchased the property, lived in the new house and renovated the barn, adding heating and cooling, to become a country music dinner playhouse bearing the same name, Vassar Playhouse. It opened around 1997, and ran about ten years, spawning several new artists in that field before closing its doors. Once again, today the property has new owners, Fred and Vicki Cooper-Foss, who plan to repair and renovate the barn for their family use. They have already begun to make nice changes to the property. May it live once again!

CPSIA information can be obtained at www.ICGtesting.com
Printed in the USA
LVOW121220281012